50
TERR
IDEAS
FOR
Cleaning
Everything

W9-BRA-151

500 TERRIFIC IDEAS FOR *Cleaning Everything*

Don Aslett

A Round Stone Press Book

A Fireside Book
Published by
SIMON & SCHUSTER INC.
NEW YORK LONDON TORONTO SYDNEY TOKYO

FIRESIDE
Simon and Schuster Building
Rockefeller Center
1230 Avenue of the Americas
New York, New York 10020

A Round Stone Press Book

Directors: Marsha Melnick, Paul Fargis, Susan E. Meyer
Design: Jeff Fitschen
Illustrations: Joe Vissichelli/Aftifax

The following brand names and products are registered
trademarks: 3M, Ajax, Biz, Capture, Carbona, Chemspec
Spot Lifter, Choreboy, Dawn, De-Solv-It, Doodlebug,
Dupont, Endust, Energine, Eureka, Fiberglass, Formica,
Formula 409, Host, Joy, K2R, Kool-aid, Limeaway,
Masslinn, Murphy's Oil soap, New Pig, Nilodor, Outright,
Pledge, Plexiglas, Q-tip, Quater, Red Out, Rubbermaid,
Rubik's Cube, Safety Foam, Saran Wrap, Scotchgard,
Scrubee Doo, Showers N'Stuff, Swisstex, Top Job,
Vaseline, Whink Carpet Stain Remover, Windex, Wisk
Power Scoop, and Woolite.

Fireside and colophon are registered trademarks of
Simon & Schuster Inc.

Manufactured in the United States of America

1 2 3 4 5 6 7 8 9 10

Library of Congress Cataloging-in-Publication Data

Aslett, Don, 1935-
    500 teriffic ideas for cleaning everything / Don Aslett.
            p.   cm.
    "A Round Stone Press Book."
    "A Fireside Book."
    ISBN 0-671-73717-1
    1. House cleaning.   I. Title.   II. Title: Five hundred
teriific ideas for cleaning everything.
TX324.A757   1991
648'.5—dc20   91-3841
                                                        CIP

CONTENTS

INTRODUCTION

When you ask a real professional how to do something, you'll be answered with a few short sentences that condense a lifetime of experience. That's what I've given you in these pages—my 35 years of frontline cleaning as a professional, including some ideas I've learned right from you at home, from your own hard-won, hands-on experience that you've shared with me.

You'll find more than a dozen of my other books out there, covering all kinds of cleaning, but this one (a book I've always wanted to do) is different. The information is all here, but it's been cast into short and sweet installments. The entries deliver big truths in small paragraphs, giving you the idea and letting you run with it.

Few of us have a whole day or week today to devote to washing or cleaning, and why should we spend more time than we need to clean our homes? If we can do something in minutes, there's no need to spend even an hour, and so I present to you minute-sized ideas.

You'll note that I do not propose clever ways to reuse pantyhose, and I don't recommend cleaning house with egg shells or peanut butter. What you'll find here are genuine professional techniques and principles. Of my 503 terrific ideas, I'd like to thank my three brightest ideas, my editorial team: Sheree Bykofsky, Carol Cartaino, and Tobi Haynes.

Because I often recommend professional supplies and equipment, the following is a rundown of the products most frequently mentioned in these pages, what they are and where to get them. Janitorial supply stores can be found almost everywhere (look in the *Yellow Pages* under that heading). Most of what you find in janitorial supply stores will clean better and for less money than the products found in supermarkets, and the professionals there will usually answer tough cleaning questions cheerfully.

Equipment and supplies

*All-purpose or neutral cleaner

A cleaner that is neither alkaline nor acid, making it safe to use on almost any surface. The best way to buy it is in concentrated form from a janitorial supply store. You'll need to mix it up yourself, but it's worth it.

*All-purpose spotter

A spot remover formulated to work on a broad range of mostly water-based spots. It's available in supermarkets, janitorial supply stores, and elsewhere under many different brand names, including Whink Carpet Stain Remover and Chemspec Spot Lifter.

*Bacteria-enzyme digester

The only effective way to deal with unpleasant organic messes such as urine and vomit, especially if they've seeped into absorbent materials such as carpet or upholstery. When you mix up the formula, it actually produces a live colony of beneficial bacteria that eats the stain- and odor-causing materials. It's available at pet stores and janitorial supply stores. One brand is called Outright, but there are others.

*Bowl cleaner

A strong acid solution especially designed to clean and remove mineral deposits from the inside of the toilet bowl; it shouldn't be used anywhere else. Bowl cleaners usually contain hydrochloric or phosphoric acid—the latter is safer though slower acting. It's available in janitorial supply stores. One brand name is Safety Foam.

*De-Solv-it

A citrus-oil-based product that will dissolve many tough stains and deposits, including gummy and sticky ones. It's available in janitorial supply stores and some supermarkets and hardware stores.

*Disinfectant cleaner

A product that cleans and disinfects at the same time. The pine cleaners available in supermarkets that contain at least 20 percent pine oil are effective disinfectant cleaners, but you can buy them in more concentrated form for less money at a janitorial supply store. A quaternary or "quat" disinfectant cleaner is best and safest for most home cleaning.

*Dry cleaning fluid or "dry spotter"

Solvent spot removers especially effective on oily and greasy stains. They're available under many brand names, including Carbona and Energine, in supermarkets, at janitorial supply stores, and elsewhere.

*Dry sponge

A thin 5x7-inch rubber sponge that resembles a giant eraser. It's used to "dry clean" walls, ceilings,
and many other surfaces. You use it until it's thoroughly dirty and then dispose of it. It's available at
janitorial supply stores.

*Dust mop treat

Usually an oily preparation that you apply to a dust
mop to increase its ability to pick up fine dust. It's
available as a liquid or spray at janitorial supply
stores and in supermarkets. Endust is one brand
name product.

*Fast-evaporating
window cleaner

Available in supermarkets with names such as
Windex, or in janitorial supply stores as concentrate. It's good for shiny surfaces such as glass and
chrome, and for other places where you want to be
especially sure not to leave a dulling film behind.

*Floor squeegee

Attached to a long handle, the floor squeegee is a
larger, heavier version of the squeegee designed to
clean windows. The better models are reversible so
that you can use them to squeegee in any direction.
A 24-inch blade is the best size for home use. It's
available at janitorial supply stores.

*Green nylon scrub pad

A moderately aggressive nylon scrubber, available
both plain and attached to a cellulose sponge; 3M
makes good ones. It's available in supermarkets
and variety stores as well as janitorial supply stores.

*Gum freeze

An aerosol product available at janitorial supply stores that you spray on chewing gum spots to "freeze" them (i.e., turn them hard and brittle) so that they can be removed easily.

*Heavy-duty cleaner/degreaser

A strong alkaline cleaner with good grease-cutting ability. Available in supermarkets as products such as Top Job and Formula 409, or in janitorial supply stores in concentrated form.

*Lambswool duster

A large puff of natural or synthetic wool on a long handle. Natural wool is best because the oils in real wool aid the dust-catching action. It's available at housewares stores and janitorial supply stores.

*Masslinn cloth

A disposable woven paper dustcloth treated with a non-oily chemical that enables it to pick up and hold dust. It's available at janitorial supply stores.

*New Pig dustcloth

A cloth made from a new fabric manufactured by Dupont. Washable and reusable, it captures and holds dust by static attraction. It's available in some grocery stores, janitorial supply stores, and hair salons.

*Oil soap

A mild, fatty soap for washing wood. Available in supermarkets and janitorial supply stores. One brand is Murphy's Oil Soap.

*Pet rake

A brush with stiff crimped bristles that does an amazing job of removing hair, fur, and fuzz from furniture, bedding, rugs, car interiors, and clothing. The most efficient pet rake is available only through Don Aslett's Cleaning Center, P.O. Box 39-J, Pocatello, ID 83204.

*Phosphoric acid cleaner

An acid that will dissolve alkaline (usually lime or calcium) deposits left on household surfaces by hard water. Limeaway and other brands are available in supermarkets, but stronger and faster acting phosphoric acid cleaners, such as Showers 'N Stuff, can be obtained at janitorial supply stores. (For home use you don't want anything above 9 percent.)

*Professional spray bottle

Refillable spray bottles that you can use to apply professional cleaning solutions that have been mixed up from concentrate. Look for sturdy, long-lasting bottles with professional quality trigger-spray heads that will withstand a lot of use. Sold in janitorial supply stores.

*Sealant

A usually transparent product that puts a permanent waterproof protective coating on concrete, tile, and other porous masonry. It's available at flooring dealers and paint stores as well as janitorial supply stores. Be sure to let the salesperson or dealer know the exact type of flooring you have and whether it's indoors or out, whether you want a matte or glossy finish, and whether you intend to wax over it.

*White nylon-faced scrub sponge

A cellulose sponge with a thin white (be sure it's white) nylon scrub pad on one side of it; 3M makes some good ones. Available at supermarkets and variety stores as well as janitorial supply stores

Any of the above items and many of the other items mentioned in this book can be ordered from Don Aslett's Cleaning Center, P.O. Box 39-J, Pocatello, ID 83204.

APPLIANCES

1 Easy come, easy go

Appliances generally are made of hard enamel and are easy to clean. For stubborn soil or hard droplets, wet the appliance well with all-purpose cleaner solution and, after a few minutes, the soil should slide off. It's neither necessary nor advised to use abrasive cleansers or steel wool.

2 Camouflage!

Those terrific orange-peel textured finishes on appliances truly free you from maintenance. Because they don't show fingerprints, smudges, and streaks, they really do require less cleaning.

3 Sticky fridge top

All refrigerators collect and hold airborne oil and dust. Next time you have a fresh sinkful of dishwater, sponge a coat of it on top of the refrigerator. Give the solution five minutes to work on the oil, and then use a paper towel to wipe off the bulk of the now half-dissolved crud. Repeat the process with a thin coat of dish soap; then wipe clean and dry.

4 Hot idea for a cold spot

The refrigerator. Even neatnicks need to take everything out of the refrigerator—including the racks—every few months to clean. Mix up a neutral cleaning solution and wash down all parts with a soft white nylon scrub sponge. Pre-wet spots of hardened food ahead of time to soften them. Dry with a clean towel.

5 Patience pays!

You've probably heard a hundred suggestions for cleaning reflector rings and burner catch pans on the stove, but listen to me. Soak them for a long time in hot dish soap solution, and scrub off the loosened stuff; then toss them back in to soak some more. Repeat. This way you end up spending only a few minutes on them altogether. Remember that heat can permanently discolor them and there's nothing you can do about it. So don't scrub your hands off trying to make them look new!

6 Coil soil

The condensation coils of your refrigerator are a handy and, in fact, *inviting* place for dust to collect, and this can pose a fire hazard, as well as make your refrigerator run less efficiently. Vacuum the fins and coils well every six months or so. You may have to pull the fridge out to do a really good job. Use the vacuum dust brush attachment of your vacuum cleaner.

7 Stubborn odor

When you just can't get an odor out of the fridge, check the rubber gasket strip. Mildew can grow and spills can go unnoticed for months in those moist little grooves and creases.

8 Cleaning those wide open spaces

Cleaning any wire rack or grill—refrigerator, oven, barbecue—in place is slow and messy and makes rinsing almost impossible, so remove them to clean. Stand them on end in the sink, and work them over with a green nylon-backed scrub sponge. Then rinse them off with the sink sprayer, and leave them to air dry.

9 One mean cleaner

Wearing rubber gloves is the first safety measure to take when cleaning the oven. Long sleeves rolled down is the next.

10 Baked is caked

When the oven won't come entirely clean with the first coat of oven cleaner, don't start scrubbing madly. Put another coat of oven cleaner on the stubborn spots and wipe gently as usual. Do this until the stubborn spots are gone and save hours of scrubbing.

11 Dimly lit

Has your oven light been gradually getting dimmer? Are you finding it harder and harder to check on the progress of the lasagna? Take a look at the appliance light. If it's coated with baked-on grease—and it probably is—take it out and carefully apply a little oven cleaner by hand to the glass part only. Put it in a dish and let the cleaner work for an hour or two before wiping it off thoroughly and drying. If you're also cleaning the oven itself, *don't* spray into the empty socket.

BASEMENTS

12 Smoother sniffing

Musty smells in the basement are usually caused by mildew, fungus, or bacteria growth. Use a disinfectant cleaner when you're cleaning the basement; you can even let a little of the solution actually dry on basement surfaces. It retards growth and cuts odors tremendously.

13 "Seal" cement

Unfinished basements are cleaned more easily when the floors are sealed. Concrete sealer is a clear, varnish-like coating available at do-it-yourself centers and janitorial supply stores. It's easy to apply. Just clean the floor thoroughly, let it dry, and apply the seal according to the directions on the label. It's just like waxing! The result will be a shiny, easy-to-sweep floor that doesn't constantly bleed off dust.

BATHROOMS

14 To the devil with damp

Excess moisture in the bathroom causes a lot of problems such as mildew, mold, and peeling paint. Use the vent fan or open the window to keep things dried out.

15 Good sink grooming

Hair in the sink or tub? Professional housekeepers dampen part of a piece of toilet paper or tissue and quickly pick up all the hair before they start their regular cleaning. It works.

16 Slow sink?

The average bathroom sink has at least a year's worth of hair and string lodged around the stopper. Hold your breath, twist the stopper, and pull. Clean the hair and slime off, replace, and watch how fast the water goes down. Now quit combing your hair over the sink!

17 Now is "wow!"

Wipe the sink and faucet in the bathroom right after you use them, when the dirt is still fresh and loose and mineral deposits haven't had a chance to accumulate. This habit is at least 87 percent more efficient than waiting until later.

18 Hi, slick!

The biggest problem with cleaning the bathroom is too much clutter—too many gadgets, bottles, and tubes out all over. Dejunk your bathroom today. Make all the unused gizmos disappear and hide as many of the useful things as possible. If you don't have hanging shelves that just encourage more clutter, you won't need to put deodorizers on them. Reducing clutter keeps the bathroom clean and free of odor-causing bacteria.

19 New tub tactics

Fiberglass and plastic tubs and shower enclosures and hot tubs aren't tough like the old porcelain and enamel ones. You'll need to clean their softer surfaces gently, with mild bathroom cleaners such as Showers 'N Stuff. Spray it on, let it sit a couple of minutes, and then, while it's still wet, scrub the surface lightly with a white nylon-faced sponge. Fixtures like these will gradually lose their sheen even if you clean them right, but it's no cause for alarm.

20 Ugly edges

The tub caulking has turned black and you're sure it isn't mildew. It won't clean off and you're right! Eighty percent of inexpensive caulking will turn black in 18 months or less. Use the most expensive silicone caulk; it pays because it won't blacken.

21 Getting to the bottom of it

Stains on the bottom of the tub aren't always removable. If the tub is old, it's probably worn out;

the porcelain or enamel over the metal is worn thin. If the steel or iron below the surface shows through and rusty stains appear, the only cure is replacement or, for a valuable tub, resurfacing.

22 Scum busting

To remove the gray coating on shower walls, you will need a two-stage attack: phosphoric acid cleaner for the mineral scale followed by a degreaser or soap scum remover for the body oil and soap scum.

23 In the "nude" for cleaning

Keep a squeegee (with a 14-inch blade) in your shower. Ten seconds of using it on the walls to remove shower fallout (soap, body oils, and hard water drops) before you step out will save hours of scrubbing later.

24 Wax 'em

If your fiberglass tub enclosure or shower walls seem to magnetically collect dirt and soap scum, they're probably badly worn and porous from too much scrubbing with abrasives and harsh chemicals. Applying a coat of car wax will put a slick, glossy finish on them that repels soap scum and hard-water deposits and makes them much easier to clean.

25 A pain in the bath

Shower doors are and always will be a pain to clean. I tore mine out and now use a simple curtain. If you aren't that aggressive, just hang an inexpensive shower curtain on the inside of the shower door. You can toss the curtain in the machine when it's dirty and the doors will stay much cleaner.

26 Shower power

If you *are* going to keep those shower doors and are stuck cleaning them, spray a mild phosphoric acid tub 'n tile cleaner, like Showers 'N Stuff, on them. Let it sit for a while to dissolve the mineral deposits, and then scrub with a white nylon scrub sponge. Rinse and dry.

27 Near miss-ion?

Improve your aim, gentlemen! Whoever cleans the floor around the toilet bowl should lightly spray the area with disinfectant cleaner, let it sit a few minutes, and then wipe it up.

28 Beat that buildup

Brushing a toilet bowl is like brushing your teeth. Do it regularly and you won't get "plaque," or in this case, hard-water buildup. It'll go far in preventing rings, too, which are also caused by hard-water deposits.

29 Bowl patrol

Don't use bleach in toilets for deep or daily cleaning. It's dangerous to you, the floor, and the fixtures. Use a disinfectant cleaner on the outside and a mild phosphoric acid cleaner on the inside, and your toilet will be not only clean but safe as well.

30 Ring relief

If you have a ring in the toilet, rub it gently with a pumice stone to remove it. Make sure the pumice is wet while you're working with it so that it won't scratch the surface. Don't use a razor blade or sandpaper—or both you and the toilet could be ruined!

31 Plastication

Saran Wrap stretched across the opening of the toilet bowl will slow down evaporation and prevent a ring over an extended period of time. Some people do this before leaving home for the winter or when they go on a long vacation to save having to clean stains when they get back. But remember to turn on the light when you return to the toilet, or the ring won't be your only problem!

32 Bowl busting

If you pour toilet bowl cleaner right into the water, the water dilutes it a hundred times. Instead, force the water out of the bowl by pushing a bowl swab quickly up and down the bowl toward the "throat" of the toilet, then wring out the swab and saturate it with full-strength cleaner. Swab it around the empty bowl, so the entire inside—even up under the rim—has the benefit of full-strength cleaner.

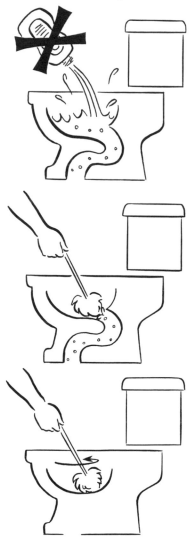

33 Blue toilets but not rugs

Those blue-water dispensers for your toilet tank do help slow down toilet soiling. When you change them, don't carry them dripping across the room or the sodium hypochlorite (chlorine bleach) that runs out of them will spot whatever it dries on. Drop those babies directly into a bucket.

34 The hang of it

Always hang the toilet paper roll so that it feeds from behind and under instead of over. This way kids and kittens are less likely to roll 80 feet of it out when they get frisky.

35 Soap

Small soap salvation! Everyone sweats out the last days of a bar of soap that's become too small to use. It slips out of your hand, out of the soap dish, breaks in half and splinters. Surely it has a few more breaths or bubbles in it, but not a whole bath or shower, and so we imagine ourselves grinding them up or gluing them together to make a bigger bar. Face it, they're dead. Wrap a bit of toilet paper around them and toss them in the wastebasket. You'll save time and guilt. Or, if you must, stick them while wet to the next bar.

36 Dual-purpose blow/dry

Smart people are putting those electric hand dryers you see in public restrooms in their bathroom. They're mounting them high so they can dry their hair without thrashing around to find the dryer. Dryers are quick, sanitary, and save on towel washing, too.

BEDS

37 Less is more

Since I have begun making the bed (my wife made it the first 20 years of our marriage, so I'm doing it for the next 20), we use one heavy quilt or comforter with a sheet under it instead of several blankets. The comforter doubles as a bedspread. I can't believe how much time it saves to not thrash around with multiple covers, and it looks good, too—if I do say so myself.

38 Catch dust napping

Bed spreads—surprise!—collect dust and dirt just like floors, carpets, and the tops of refrigerators. If you don't believe me, just slap one the next time you walk by. So occasionally, as you vacuum, set your upright vacuum right up on the bed and vacuum the spread. Amazing!

CARPETS

39 Cleaner colors

After 32 years of professional carpet cleaning, I can tell you that the best-looking carpets after 10 years of wear tend to be textured, multi-hued patterns, in medium tones of red or rust. The worst looking carpets are solid in color, either extremely dark or light; the very worst are light blue, white, or yellow. Think of that when you're out buying carpet.

40 Nothing like nylon

What carpet is easiest to keep clean? Nylon, no doubt about it.

41 Soft but sorry!

Don't carpet a bathroom! Grooming residue and the inevitable toilet misses and bowl overflows are too hard to clean out of a fuzzy floor; moreover, the warmth and moisture in a bathroom encourage things that you don't even want to think about to grow on a bathroom carpet.

42 "Pretty" painful

As I advise for bathrooms, I'd avoid carpet in kitchens. It may look and feel good, but it's 100 percent guaranteed to collect food spills, which take 10 times longer to clean out of carpet than tile. Carpeting also offers germs a great place to live, breed, and create odors.

43 Stalling shampooing

There's no way to keep carpet from collecting dust and dirt from foot traffic, spills, and airborne soil. Eventually it will need shampooing. Two practices that will help stave off shampooing as long as possible are (1) regular vacuuming and (2) using good walkoff mats at every entrance, both inside and out.

44 Carpeted walls

You've probably heard of carpeting walls either one-half or all the way. I did it once and loved it. Carpet doesn't chip; kids won't write on it; and it requires almost no cleaning. It also absorbs sound and is a real maintenance-free idea.

45 Surface slicking

For quick cleanup of surface carpet dirt, get a big, heavy cotton towel or use a clean dust mop. Dip the mop or towel in carpet shampoo solution, wring it as dry as possible, and rub it over the carpet. The cotton towel or mop head will pick up the dirt and absorb the soils out of the nylon or wool of the carpet. Change to a clean side of the towel or mop and rinse as necessary; repeat until you or the carpet dirt give out.

46 To clean or not to clean

You can determine if it's time to shampoo a carpet by comparing a saved remnant with what's down on the floor. If you don't have a remnant, feel the carpet. If it's matted and sticky, it needs cleaning.

47 Shampoo

Before you shampoo a carpet, always vacuum it extra well before you start. It will only take a few minutes and will improve the quality and speed of the shampooing job by up to 50 percent.

48 Easy release

Pre-spraying is important when shampooing carpet. This is the process of lightly spraying or misting your carpet with a cleaning solution (an all-purpose cleaner works fine) five minutes before you plan to clean it. Use a regular spray bottle or, if you have a lot of carpet, a weed sprayer. The pre-spraying will soften and release the surface oil and dirt.

49 Blocking

After cleaning, spotting, or in any way dampening carpets, never set furniture down directly on the wet carpet. That would either rust the carpet or cause the wood to stain it. Instead, place a small piece of cardboard about two inches square under each leg. Make sure there's no printing on the cardboard, or the resulting ink stain will thwart your efforts.

50 Too much moisture

Occasionally when we clean a carpet—especially an older carpet—the carpet ends up with a big, dark yellowish stain that can't be scrubbed out. This is called "browning"; the moisture and cleaning chemicals have caused the jute backing to release some of its color. If that happens, call a professional rug cleaner; they have a browning acid that will convert the color back to normal.

51 All dried up

Carpet pile will dry the way it's left when you finish shampooing, and if you're not careful about how you leave it, it will reflect light differently and look streaky. Before it dries you should "rake" the pile with a carpet rake or a bamboo leaf rake. You can even use a broom for this. Just be sure the nap is all standing or lying the same way, and then let it dry.

52 Powder it clean

Can you dry clean carpet? Yes! There are two products we professionals use: Host and Capture. Both are white fibers impregnated with a cleaning agent. Use as directed: "spread the formula over the carpet without wetting; work in with a brush." Then use a good upright vacuum cleaner with a beater bar to pull out the contaminated cleaner. It's work. But it works!

53 Shrink proofing

Wool carpet will usually shrink when it's cleaned; how much will depend on how wet you get it. Before you clean it, check the tack strip around the edge and make sure the carpet is down and gripped well by the little slanted teeth. If it's well gripped, it's less likely to pull off when it shrinks.

54 Foil resoiling

Is your just-cleaned carpet or upholstery resoiling too fast? Ninety-five percent of this is caused by shampoo residue left in the carpet due to inadequate rinsing; the residue attracts dust and dirt like a magnet. Carpet needs to be rinsed extremely well after cleaning. An extractor and plain hot water will do the job just fine.

55 Cow catcher

"Cow trails" won't develop in your carpet as quickly if you apply some soil retardant to the high traffic areas when the carpet is new, or right after it's been shampooed. The chemical coats the fibers and keeps stains and soil from penetrating.

CLEANERS

56 Home brew

If you're really into home brew, it's possible to mix your own cleaners at home. But if you just want safe, workable, economical products, stick with commercial cleaners. You can't make cleaners as well or as cheaply as you can buy them.

57 Water alone won't do it

Plain water does very little cleaning. It will rinse and flood, but you need to use soap, detergent, or other surfactant to penetrate and "lift" dirt.

58 Go straight to the source

Shop for professional cleaning supplies at your local janitorial supply store. Concentrated commercial products save money because they're less expensive than supermarket brands; they save time because they generally work better and faster and last longer; and they save room because they come in small packets. Just look in the *Yellow Pages* under Janitorial Supply.

59 Concentrate!

There are many great all-purpose cleaners on supermarket shelves, but why not buy some all-purpose cleaner concentrate at the janitorial supply store and mix it with your own water in your own spray bottle. It'll work just as well and save you money, and you'll have to buy cleanser much less often.

60 Just a bit

"If a little is good, a lot is better"—wrong! Dilute cleaners according to directions. A too-strong mix can damage surfaces and may actually destroy the dirt-cutting and suspending action of the chemical. Too much soap in window-washing water, for example, is what causes streaks; and mopping waxed floors with overly strong cleaners will dull and soften the wax.

61 Water first

When mixing up cleaners from concentrate, fill the bottle with water before you add the cleaner concentrate to avoid producing inches of foam. This will prevent chemical splashes, too.

62 pH pointer

Grease is acid, and so a cleaner such as ammonia or another heavy-duty cleaner from the opposite end of the pH scale—alkaline—is needed to dissolve it. The more alkaline a cleaner, the more grease-cutting power it has.

63 Spraying pays

Use commercial trigger-spray bottles for cleaning

instead of aerosols. They are safer for the environment and for you.

64 Get tough with grease

For those really tough grease-removal jobs, go to your janitorial supply store and get some degreaser. It won't hurt the porcelain on appliances, but be careful with it on plastic or paint. It may do damage if mixed too strong or left on too long.

65 A snort for cleaning

Alcohol is a great solvent for dissolving grease, inks, and other stains. Neither drinking nor rubbing alcohol works well, however, because they contain sugar, fragrance, or excess water that may promote stain. Go to the drugstore and get a half pint of "pure" (91 percent) alcohol and keep it on hand for grease stains.

66 Coating caution!

All those magic coatings people put on things, such as silicones, oils, and waxes, seem to work great until the coating goes sour or gets soiled. Now you have two problems, the coating and the original surface! Whenever you can, learn how to clean an item or surface, not coat it.

67 Watch those abrasives

Just because a cleanser is soft and wet, doesn't mean it won't scratch. Imagine wet sandpaper. Avoid any cleanser—wet or dry—that is abrasive.

This warning even includes toothpaste. Abrasives tend to eat up the surface of fixtures, counters, and anything else you dare to use them on.

68 Mercy!

Scouring powder does just what it says: scours. But if you're not careful, it will remove surfaces—such as paint, finish, and platings. The drier you scour, the worse it is!

69 Sad shower

Take it easy when cleaning with bleach! It oxidizes and damages many surfaces. Bleach removes the color from things and gives the illusion that it's cleaning, but it isn't; it's just bleaching.

70 Clean before you disinfect

It's important to clean *before* you disinfect; otherwise the dirt will interfere with the action of the disinfectant, or totally prevent it from working.

71 A bad mix

NEVER mix ammonia and bleach while cleaning. It creates deadly chlorine gas that has taken many a life!

72 Minor league bleaching

Three percent hydrogen peroxide is the safest

bleach to use when you're not sure if an item or surface can withstand bleaching. Try it before going to the "big guns," such as chlorine bleach.

73 Smells clean, too!

Pine cleaners that contain 20 percent or more real pine oil are good cleaners and sanitizers. To sanitize, let the solution sit for several minutes on the surface before you flush or wipe it off.

74 Polish folly

Stick to one brand and type of polish once you find one that you like, and if you want to experiment use different rags for each type. Don't keep pouring different kinds of polish onto the same old rag. Mixing polish is the surest way to cloud and streak the finish.

75 Not-fast food

The reason lemon and vinegar work on mild lime or calcium buildups that result from using hard water is because they are acids, which are on the opposite end of the pH scale from the alkaline deposits you're trying to remove. These "edible" cleaners, however, are only about a tenth as effective as phosphoric acid mineral-scale removers.

76 No magic

Baking soda is a great odor neutralizer, but it's not necessarily a cleaner. It has no soap or surfactant to release and rinse away soils. But don't be disappointed; baking soda still works great in the fridge.

77 Good old salt

Salt is not a cleaner. It can help cleaning by serving as a poultice, or absorber, for some liquid spills such as blood. It sucks it up and holds the spill so that it won't spread. But don't scrub with it; sprinkle it, and then sweep it away.

78 Vinegar and water

Vinegar isn't a cleaner either, but it's a great rinsing agent. It neutralizes alkaline detergents and leaves surfaces nice and shiny and residue free. A white vinegar and water rinse is great on floors, after they've been cleaned with a real cleaner. Any wax you apply after this treatment will stick and stay better because any leftover residue from the cleaner will be gone.

79 A countertop cavity!

Using toothpaste to clean house will get you down in the mouth. It doesn't have much dirt-dissolving power, and it is a mild abrasive. In most cases it'll leave a white "scrub patch" behind on the surface of whatever you use it on. For stubborn marks and stains, use all-purpose cleaner on a wet nylon scrub pad instead.

80 Kill time

Disinfectants need time to kill those bad "bugs." So when you spray disinfectant cleaner on bathroom fixtures and other surfaces to kill germs and retard mildew, leave the surface moist with the cleaner for several minutes before you wipe it off to be sure you get them all.

81 Poison their pad

On odor- or mildew-prone surfaces, lightly spray another mist of disinfectant cleaner over the surface after you've cleaned it, and just let it dry. This will leave an unfriendly atmosphere for bacteria and mildew.

82 Outdated

Kerosene, turpentine, and naphtha are old solvents once well received in cleaning circles. But they're as likely to create stains as to take them out, and they're smelly and highly flammable. Use dry cleaning solvents from the supermarket or janitorial supply store instead and get rid of any half-used cans of outdated solvent.

83 A hard-to-beat hand cleaner!

In my welding and machine shop at home I have lots of he-man hand cleaners, but nothing is as convenient and works as well on my hands as a plain old dish detergent such as Dawn.

84 Secure the soil

In the old days, the sandman was a cleaner! He sold sand to people to sprinkle on their floors to absorb grease, oils, and soil. The dirty sand was then swept up and away. Sawdust, sand, and even kitty litter have the same type of absorbency and are good choices for absorbing and removing the bulk of messy liquid spills and soils. Just sprinkle one of these materials over the spill, let it do its job, and remove it.

CLEANING TECHNIQUES

85 Where to start

Don't touch a mop, broom, dust cloth, or vacuum until you've straightened up the area to be cleaned. Get rid of the good, bad, and the ugly: put your good things where they go, store or remove un-needed items and clutter, and trash the trash. It'll make things look better immediately and save you a lot of time when you get down to the business of cleaning.

86 Here and there

Don't keep trying to find chunks of time to do the cleaning. If you just take advantage of the five-, ten-, and fifteen-minute time fragments that come your way every day, you may never have to spend all day Saturday cleaning again. Take advantage of those TV commercials, phone calls that leave your hands free, waiting time, etc.

87 Skip cleaning

Even professionals regularly skip parts of usual cleaning routines when no cleaning is warranted. If only heavily trafficked areas are littered, don't both-er to vacuum the clean, untouched areas; if Aunt Emma with her white gloves already visited this year, skip dusting the knickknack shelves; if no one even goes into the guest room, you don't need to either every time you clean.

88 The psychology of scrubbing

The scientific name for elbow grease is "agitation," which means rubbing or scrubbing a surface to help pull the soil loose and to help the cleaning solution penetrate. We agitate whenever we have stubborn dirt where the solution alone won't cut it. But begin agitating carefully at first to be sure the finish can take it.

89 Strategic scrubbing

Always scrub in four directions: north/south, and east/west; that way you get the surface from all sides. Sure beats scrubbing in a circle!

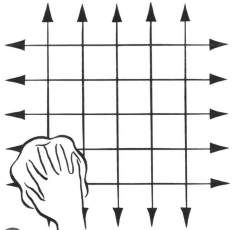

90 Wetting

When cleaning, too many of us don't realize the importance of "wetting," which means being sure the solution penetrates instead of rolling around on the surface (like plain water on a waxed car). If the cleaning solution doesn't penetrate, it won't clean. If that's the case, take one or all of these steps: (1) change your solution (the one you have may not be suited to the job); (2) remix the solution, and be sure you get the ratio right this time; or (3) ask a pro about the problem surface.

91 Soften your life

If you live in a hard-water area, softening your water can do a lot to simplify cleaning. With soft water you'll use less soap and detergent, and you won't have to work to get up a lather. Hard-water scale clogs up pipes, coats shower walls, and creates rings in the toilet. It grays laundry and coats it with soap scum. Hard-water deposits often damage household surfaces and are tough to remove. Soft water causes none of these problems.

92 Soak, don't scrub

Soaking is the key to cleaning. It lets the cleaning solution have time to work so *you* don't have to. Most rubbing and scrubbing and (do I have to say it?) scouring is wasted motion. Just let the solution sit and work for a minute, and the surface will practically come clean by itself (and be left undamaged, too).

93 Chore person

Old hardened spatters are a lot tougher to clean than new soil and will seldom wipe off easily. I recommend curly metal Choreboy pads and a dish detergent solution to clean old dirt; they have hundreds of little "blades" that won't hurt the surface if you keep the pad wet while you're working with it. They'll tenderly slice through all of those old built-up spatters, even greasy ones. Be sure to rinse that little helper well when you are done.

94 Tub flub

Don't use your bathtub to wash oven grills, blinds, vents, etc. in strong cleaning solutions. The newer tubs especially can be damaged by even strong solutions of ammonia or heavy-duty cleaner. A lot of tubs are ruined that way.

95 The right pace

When you're cleaning walls, floors, windows, or anywhere else, spread the cleaning solution in quantities that suit your speed and reach. To avoid messy streaks, you need to go back and remove each application before it dries.

96 The wall chill factor

Should you choose hot or cold cleaning solutions?

Hot or warm water does dissolve soap, detergent, and soil better, but keep in mind that as soon as the solution hits the floor, walls, or windows, it's soon room temperature anyway. So don't fry your fingernails trying to boil the dirt off.

97 Too dirty?

You can determine when it's time to clean the mop or change the cleaning water by scooping up a handful of the solution. If you can't see your palm through the water, change it.

98 Get rid of that residue

Don't forget to rinse. Some of the chemicals (usually alkaline) we use to loosen and lift soil are often left behind on the "clean" surface. This residue causes streaks and cuts the shine. Flushing or flooding well with water right after cleaning will wash the residue away. A touch of white vinegar in the rinse water neutralizes alkalinity and leaves the surface *really* clean.

99 Choosing spray bottles

Quart-sized spray bottles are more efficient than pint-sized ones. They hold more and don't tip over so easily; furthermore, they make it simpler to measure concentrated liquids that require diluting.

100 Nozzle know-how

Adjusting the nozzle on spray bottles to fit the situation not only speeds up cleaning, it saves lives. Out in open areas a spray bottle can be set for misting.

In a confined area like a shower or closet, set the nozzle to stream. That will prevent you from inhaling chemical fog.

101 Color-code 'em

Make sure all of your cleaning spray bottles are transparent so that you can see how much solution is in each and what color it is. Always use the same color of each type of cleaner—the whole family will know by looking what they're using. The pros tend to choose: blue—window cleaner; green—all-purpose cleaner; red or pink—disinfectant cleaner.

102 Wringing

Never wring sponges; just squeeze them. They'll last longer and hold their shapes better.

103 Don't be a sponge

A sponge won't drip on you if you don't dip it in the cleaning solution any deeper than a quarter of its thickness.

104 Sponge size

Are those giant sponges soaking you when you use them or try to squeeze them out? Does the liquid run down your arm and into your shoe? Either buy the right size to begin with or with a scissor, razor blade, or good kitchen bread knife, cut them down to fit your hand.

105 Sponge care

Sponges tend to get discolored with use. Don't worry about it, it's natural. Just rinse them well after each use to flush away germs, and they'll be fine. Whatever you do, don't bleach them, or they'll deteriorate fast.

106 More sponge care

Even the best high-quality sponges, natural or synthetic, live only so long. When they get brittle, stained, smelly, or start falling apart, pull the plug on 'em—or they'll begin to leave more debris than they pick up.

107 Faster drying

Whenever you use lots of moisture to clean carpet or anything else, remember that most rooms hold moisture, which can then condense onto all of the room's surfaces. I've seen moisture loosen wall covering and untune pianos. Even on cold days, always open doors and windows for a while when you're doing wet cleaning; this will help to dry things out and eliminate odors. Turning up the heat just recycles stale air.

108 Drying time

When wax, paint, or concrete sealer is dry to the touch, it may not be *totally* dry. Give it a little longer before recoating the surface or otherwise disturbing it. You won't be sorry. A smooth surface is always easier to clean than one that has nicks and irregularities in it.

109 "Cool" it!

The best room temperature to clean your house by is 60°! Set your thermostat at 60° so you can work up a little sweat while you clean without getting overheated.

110 Over clean

Deep cleaning (some people call it spring cleaning) is only necessary if you're hard on your home. Deep cleaning every three years is enough for a new or lightly used home. Too many people fail to consider the soil level and instead deep clean by habit, schedule, or tradition.

111 Fall cleaning

Fall, not spring, is the best time to do deep cleaning. Most dirt will penetrate your home, especially your carpet, during the spring and summer when windows are more likely to be open and kids and pets spend more time outdoors increasing traffic. Getting the dirt out in early fall will save wear and tear on everything all winter. And your home will be nice and clean for the holidays.

112 No about face!

When you're dust mopping, always lead with the same edge and move the dust mop in a serpentine pattern rather than in a straight line. This technique takes full advantage of the nap that forms as a dust mop is used. Don't lift the head from the floor until you're finished or you'll lose your dust load.

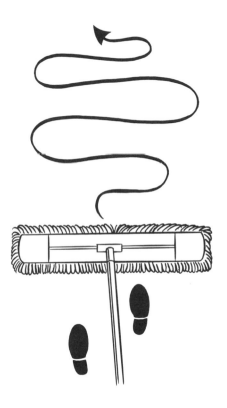

113 Odor removal

Air fresheners don't really get rid of odor, they just mask it. The only way to get rid of an odor is to find and get rid of the source. As long as the source of the problem remains, there will always be an odor.

CLUTTER

114 Shed secrets

The contents of the average backyard shed are so sacred, so complex, and so mystifying, that only the owner (you!) knows what and how to clean here. I suggest you make a cleaning sweep of the shed once a month to scoop off the hulls and culls. Most people try to do it yearly and are so discouraged that they can't face it again for another five years. Do it monthly with a garbage can at hand and you'll stay even.

115 The closet cure

The best closet cleaning cure is to dejunk. There are some great new closet organizers now, but remember, organized junk is still junk. Closets weren't made for clutter!

116 Cleaner closets

Use hard enamel paint inside your closets when you repaint so that shoe scuffs and hanger marks can be cleaned off easily. Flat paints only encourage closet clutter mess.

117 Clothes closet clutter

Clothing we no longer wear is one of the biggest sources of junk and clutter. (There are thousands of postmenopausal women reading this right now who still have their maternity clothes!) Plan an annual or semi annual trip to your neighborhood Goodwill.

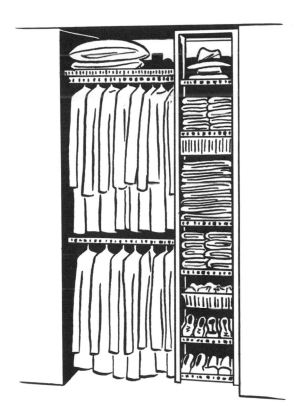

118 Bag it and brag!

Are you always cleaning up kids' school papers? A Utah mother posts the best on the bulletin board, and as soon as it's out of date, replaces it with a fresh one. This gets all the value out of them without creating a stockpile. Okay—save a *few* of the most notable for posterity and send one or two on to the grandparents.

119 Subscription clutter

At least one-third of our "libraries" (book collections) and three-fourths of the magazines laying around the house are useless clutter. They slow down cleaning and build up guilt. Toss them today and you'll save housecleaning time and lots of room.

120 Round up and put up

The key to a happy and healthy hobby room (sewing room or shop) is organization. After you've policed the house and rounded them all up, your tools and equipment need to be separated and hung up or neatly drawered, ready to use. That means find a handy, logical place for everything. Nothing should ever be sitting on the workbench itself.

DOORS

121 Hand held

Doorknobs are the dirtiest place in the house. Spray them and a 10-inch area around them with all-purpose cleaner solution. Let it sit for a minute to dissolve the dirt, and then wipe it off with a terry cloth. You'll be shocked at the difference, and they'll be sanitized.

122 Dust heaven

I always sand and varnish or paint the tops of my doors, even though they don't show. But they do collect a lot of dust and grease. If the top is sealed and smooth it cleans fast, and dustcloths don't snag on the door top.

123 Dealing with dust

There is often as much dust on the sides of a door frame or casing as there is on the top. Static cling occurs where air is sucked through the crack around the door, and dust builds up there. So don't forget to dust the entire frame!

124 Scuff busting

Most of those black marks on the bottom of a door will be tough to get off because they're kicked on. Use a green nylon scrub sponge and all-purpose cleaner solution. Get the sponge good and wet and scrub carefully. Dry immediately with a clean cloth.

125 Don't over door it

Mounting things on doors may be handy, but it generally creates long-range problems. Door hinges and doors are designed to support the weight of opening and closing them, not for carrying heavy shelves or racks of shoes. Use the wall or dejunk!

DRAINS

126 Ugh!

If the water in your sink is going down too slowly, 90 percent of the time you'll find that the culprit is buildup on the stopper. Sometimes, too, the plumber will leave a slight burr or metal shaving when reaming pipes. When not removed, the shaving may accelerate buildup. Regardless of the original cause, wet hair always catches on the slow stoppers, and when soap adds to the buildup, the stopper continues to catch other things as well. You can twist many stoppers to remove them; if not, turn off the water, unscrew the lever under the sink, and pull out the stopper. Be prepared for a gruesome surprise. Clean the stopper well, rinse, and replace it.

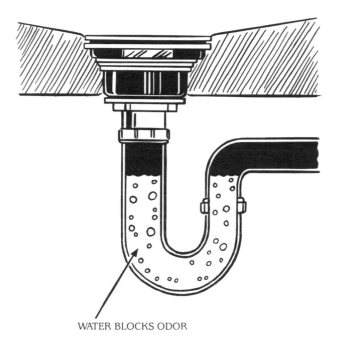

WATER BLOCKS ODOR

127 Drain sense

Floor drains have a hidden "S" trap that's meant to hold water and block sewer odors. Water in the trap, however, can become old and stale or even evaporate when the drain isn't used often. Every month or so, pour a bucket of water with a little pine cleaner added to it into the drain to keep it fresh and odor-free.

DUST

128 Capture!

Feather dusters do knock dust off gently; however, they don't pick it up. Use a Masslinn dusting cloth or lambswool duster (both available at janitorial supply stores). Both have a magnetic quality that captures and holds the dust.

129 Dust or vacuum first?

You dust first! This knocks the fallen leaves, orange pits, dead insects, even fingernail clippings onto the floor so the vacuum can get them.

130 Spider power!

Cobwebs come off easily if you pick them off rather than rub them in. The lambswool duster (a woolen fluff ball that looks like cotton candy on a stick) is the best tool for the purpose. Extension handles are available for them for high reaches.

131 Dust opera

You should probably dust the front of the TV more often than you do now. The static electricity there is a magnet for dust. You'll be surprised at how much you will collect when you start wiping it down a couple of times a week.

132 Hop to it!

Dust bunnies (that soft, light collection of lint, hair, and fuzz under you bed) are relatively harmless. So relax, and when you are so moved to clean them and can't get your upright vacuum under there all the way, park it close by and sweep the bunnies toward it. The suction and their lightness will invite them to hop right in.

133 Dust busting

To help alleviate the effects of dust allergies while cleaning: (1) install professional quality walkoff mats at every entrance to capture and contain the dust; (2) change the vacuum bag and furnace filter more often; and (3) get a built-in central vacuum, or even a water-circulating vacuum, which removes more dust than a regular vac, by eliminating the blowing end of the vac, which stirs up room dust and distributes the fine dust that inevitably escapes the bag.

DUST MOPS

134 Opt for the mop

A dust mop is more efficient for your hard-surface floors than a bristle broom. Whereas brooms leave small particles behind and kick dust up into the air to be redeposited, a treated dust mop collects and holds even the finest dust.

135 Treat it right

To treat a dust mop, spray it generously with En-dust or a commercial dust mop oil. Roll it up like a sock and place in a plastic bag for 12 to 24 hours. This will allow the "treatment" to penetrate through the whole head and be distributed evenly so that it can catch and hold those dust bunnies.

136 Heads up and out

Never store your dust mop with the head down on the floor or lean it against the wall; that would transfer the oily dust treatment onto the floor or wall. Hang or store the mop with the handle down and the face out.

137 Floor-care partners

Vacuum your dust mop occasionally to pull the fuzz and fur out of it. The mop will be cleaner and much more efficient.

EMERGENCY CLEANING

138 A hot lead!

If you have any kind of a fire at home—be it caused by a frying pan or furnace—before you clean, call your insurance agent. Fire insurance generally covers all such fire emergencies, and sometimes they'll have a pro totally clean the mess for you.

139 "Float" it dry

If you have any kind of a flood, call a carpet restoration crew; they will use a blower under your carpets that "floats" them dry. A thoroughly wet carpet never dries well from the top down. Without blowing, the underside will rot and mildew.

140 Instant company

People will be here in five minutes and the house is a fright: (1) clean the entranceway; (2) clean yourself (put on lipstick or a clean shirt); (3) turn up the lights (brightness gives the illusion of cleanliness); (4) lock the pets in another room; (5) don't apologize (imagine what theirs looks like!).

FLOORS

141 Pile pickup

To pick up those final floor sweepings that are too fine for the lip of the dust pan, I just quickly wet (and have been known to lick) a piece of paper and whisk it over the pile. The fine grit sticks to the paper like glue.

142 Scrubbing scripture

Hands and knees are a thing of the past. Any floor tool that won't accommodate a handle isn't worth owning! Aslett 6:21.

143 Non-stick floor

If you have a sticky kitchen floor, it's because you haven't managed to cut and remove the dirt and grease. Just a touch of dishwashing detergent (Joy, Dawn, etc.) in your mop water will dissolve and release that clinging soil. Plain water or vinegar water won't do it. Vinegar and cooking grease are both mild acids. Dish soap is an alkali and will neutralize grease.

144 Two passes, please!

You mop a floor faster and better when you make two passes. First, take a quick trip over it to spread the solution and wait a few minutes for it to dissolve the soil. Then, wring your mop dryer and mop more carefully to remove the dirt.

145 The rule of thumb

When you strip the floor, scrape it with your fingernail or a kitchen utensil to tell if the old wax is softened and off or not. If nothing gathers under your nail, the floor is wax free.

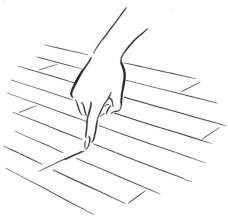

146 Safer stepping

Wax will make a floor less slippery, not more slippery. Wax and floor finish serve like light, flexible cushions that absorb friction on the floor.

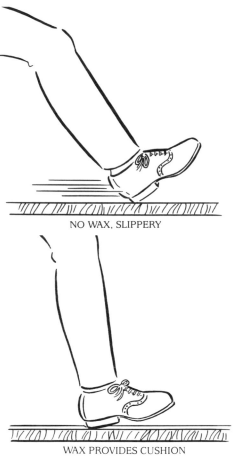

NO WAX, SLIPPERY

WAX PROVIDES CUSHION

147 No no-wax floor?

Your no-wax floor needs waxing? Sad, but true, a no-wax floor is like a no-wash dish: it doesn't exist! No wax is great in theory, but it works only on TV. Every floor needs a protective finish to stay new-looking forever and to protect it from abrasion.

148 It's the pits

If a floor surface is designed with a lot of little indentations and relief lines, generally the first scrubbing won't get all the dirt and old wax out. Instead of taking the old toothpick approach, just go over the entire floor again with a fresh batch of cleaning solution. This will generally reach the hidden dirt and lift it out. If necessary, a nylon scrub brush will get down into "the pits" where your mop has missed.

149 The right spots

When applying wax or finish, give the whole area onc coat; then apply the second coat in the traffic areas only and not under things. This prevents wax from building up in areas where it won't have a chance to be worn off.

150 Powdering

If your floor wax powders, it means that either you let it dry too fast or you put a hard wax over a previous application of soft wax or you waxed over soap or detergent residue. When you determine what you did, desist!

151 Rinse

Your floor won't shine like it should if soap residue remains after mopping. If you use lots of detergent to get it clean, then you should put some white vinegar in your rinse water to neutralize the alkalinity and to avoid accumulating residue that will absorb light and subdue the shine.

152 Forget the Jones's floor

Some floors are much easier to maintain than others, usually because they're more expensive or have a more reflective surface. So don't break your back trying to match your neighbor's kitchen or the bank's lobby floor. Inexpensive floors and some colors are almost impossible to make look good.

153 Easy-off marks

Black marks on the floor are easily removed if the floor is waxed. Then the marks are on the wax, not the surface of the floor. Rub lightly with a damp white nylon pad and the top thin layer of wax will come off with the black mark. If the floor isn't waxed and you rub hard, you'll take off part of the floor and leave an ugly white or matte-finish spot. Bad news! That's one more good reason to apply wax or finish to a floor.

154 Floor registers

Anything floor-mounted gets the worst beating a home has to offer. When vacuuming doesn't do much for floor grills and grates, pull them out, and soak them in a bucket of all-purpose cleaning solution. Then scrub them with a brush, rinse, air dry, and replace.

155 Down with double brushes

When you're sure you need a floor buffer at home, the single-disc models are at least twenty times better than the double-brush units. Watch the classified section of your paper and you might find a 12- or

13-inch commercial unit that normally sells for hundreds of dollars at a fraction of the cost.

156 Better buffing

Buffing is simply smoothing the surface of anything enough to cause light to be reflected instead of absorbed! For better buffing, the new white nylon pads on floor machines beat the old lambswool and cloth bonnets hands down.

157 Punctured floors

Spiked high heels are one of the biggest enemies of floors. A 110-pound woman can exert 2,000 pounds of point-of-impact pressure with these. Not surprisingly, high heels leave holes and indentations in wood, tile, and sheet vinyl. Those heel points also make powder of wax and polyurethane. Damaged shoes (those with the rubber heel tip loose or missing) do the most damage. Examine the tips of your shoes and either fix or fling them. If you really want to save wear and tear on your floors, take high heels off at home when you can. You'll probably find you'll be more comfortable too.

158 Floor face-lift

Asphalt floor tile is old news now. Most of it is tired and porous, but some of it is still in good shape. To spiff it up, first use wax stripper to strip it down. It will look dry after that because it is. Go to a janitorial supply store and buy some asphalt tile restorer. Apply as directed. It'll put life and glow back into the floor and, best of all, will provide a light new surface to wax over and clean. That tile should last another 10 or 20 years!

159 Yellowing

You may discover a yellowed spot under an area rug. This may be from old discolored wax, or it may be that the hidden area is a different color be-cause it has not been exposed to ultraviolet rays of sunlight, which the rest of the floor has received. If stiff scrubbing with a white nylon-backed sponge doesn't start removing it fast, it probably isn't going to come out, so stop now or you'll end up with a *rough,* yellowed surface. Try relocating the rug to see if the spot disappears by itself after a few months.

FURNITURE

160 Overkill

Furniture's biggest problem is accumulation of too much gunky polish. Use less, and use it less often.

161 Wood wash

Stop! Don't "Pledge" and polish your furniture to death. If it needs cleaning, wash it with an oil soap made for wood, such as Murphy's—that's what re-moves fingerprints, grease, and flyspecks. Then buff it dry with a terry towel to bring out the luster in the forty coats of polish probably already on it.

162 Leave it off the lacquered stuff

Lemon oil or other penetrating and conditioning oils for wood do very little good on varnished or lacquered wood furniture. In fact they're mostly a liability, as the oil can't reach the actual wood. It just sits on top of the varnish and attracts dust. Penetrating oil meant to be used on bare, thirsty, unfinished wood.

163 Stays sticky

Linseed oil isn't a cleaner or a polish. It's a penetrant to condition and protect bare wood. If you use it on polished furniture, it won't dry and will collect dust and double your cleaning time.

164 Antiques

Wood that's "antique" is generally old and dry, and the varnish or other protective coating is often worn away in spots. Use water sparingly, with a mild oil soap, then think about sealing the piece in question with Urethane or oil.

165 A perfect blend

After you've cleaned your furniture, nicks or worn spots might show. Some books say to use walnut meats or iodine or shoe polish, but that's too complicated, and too uncertain. Go to the paint store and get a set of furniture crayons. They're easy to use, last longer, and the selection allows you a real color match, not just a darkened spot.

166 Patience pays

Ninety-five percent of the time beverage rings on wood furniture are caused by moisture condensing from a hot or cold drink and reacting with the varnish. Many will go away by themselves if you just leave them alone for a few days. If the ring isn't too deep, you can gently sand and refinish to get rid of the ring.

167 Upholstery spots

After spot cleaning upholstered furniture, shampoo the whole panel the spot was on to prevent water spots and rings.

168 Neat seat

Furniture cushions are what catch most of the spills and sweat. Most upholstery seats now can be removed and taken to the dry cleaner.

169 Scotchgard

Most new upholstery fabrics are treated with "Scotchgard" or soil retardant. However, as you clean armrests and headrests (the most dirt-prone areas), the protection will gradually wear off, so be sure to re-treat these areas every time you deep clean them.

170 The secret of shampooing

You can clean or shampoo your own upholstery. I recommend hand scrubbing with an upholstery shampoo, but make sure you remove all the soap residue. Just scraping off the visible foam is not enough; use a supermarket rental extractor and rinse it. With a machine like this you can shoot water in and vacuum 95 percent of it back out. This flushes out the residue and leaves the upholstery fresh. Then follow with Scotchgard.

171 For that well-groomed look

When you finish shampooing or spot cleaning upholstery and napped fabrics, especially velvet, brush the pile all in one direction. Don't leave it to dry with the fibers matted down; it may get clean, but it will look bad!

172 Glide ride

To move furniture without scratching the floor, tilt the unit to lift each leg an inch and lay a towel or similar pad under it, then pull the pad as you move the unit.

173 Mink oil

Mink oil is great for your cowhide boots, but think twice before putting it on leather upholstery. It smells and attracts some insects (and mink!).

174 Lather that leather

I use saddle soap to clean my baseball mitts, leather cases, and leather furniture. Work up a head of lather and wipe on just the suds with a soft cloth. Work it in well and wipe it off again as many times as you need to until all the soil is gone. Your leather will be clean and a lot more supple.

KITCHEN

175 Super scrubber

Doing dishes by hand? Recently I found a new tool that beats any dishwasher around. It's a two-inch-thick sponge with a coarse nylon face that really goes after dried-on food. It's made by Swiss-tex. If you can't find one, write to me at P.O. Box 39, Pocatello, ID 83204.

176 Prepping the pots

When you're handwashing dishes, fill those crusted pots with fresh dish detergent solution before you start on the easier stuff. By the time you get to the pots, the surfactants in the solution will have done half of the work for you.

177 Metal marks

Black marks on pots, dishes, and the sink (a common complaint) generally result from contact with metal utensils. Black marks are not easy to clean, but rubbing a white nylon scrub sponge vigorously over the spots while they're wet will remove them.

178 For a clean cut

Wooden chopping blocks are outlawed in public kitchens now because of the health risk associated with bacteria lodging in the wood. If you still have one and love it, it can be cleaned with a nylon scrub sponge and dish detergent solution and then wiped dry. After it's good and dry, treat it with a little mineral oil.

179 Crumbs

Keeping a little hand vacuum near crumby areas is the best approach yet to crumb recovery. Try to pick the crumbs up while they're dry and still in one spot.

180 Not so slick

Kitchen cabinets and some drawers—even nice wooden ones—tend to accumulate oil slicks around the handle grips. Sponge on some fresh dishwater, wait a minute or two, and then quickly polish dry. Wood "cleaners" and oils won't clean kitchen cabinets as well as dishwashing liquid and water.

181 Starting at the top

Plastic laminate (Formica) countertops are wonderful, but they do wear out over the years, allowing some stains that used to wipe off to now penetrate.

Most such stains will fade after a while if you just clean off the worst of it and leave it alone. Aggressive scrubbing just wears the surface out faster. Likewise, bleaching takes the color out, not the stain, and also oxidizes the surface. Apply a little dish detergent solution to the spot, let it sit a few minutes, and finish with a whisk of your white nylon scrub sponge if necessary. Then dry with a towel. Trust me, the rest of the grape juice will fade away with daily washing.

182 Grimeless grip

Cabinets without handles are easier to clean. When replacing your old cabinets, building a new house, or remodeling, choose cabinets that have a grip opening underneath. Believe it or not, this will save you months of time cleaning cabinets over your lifetime.

183 Pest control

Bugs, beetles, ants, and all their relatives have a hard time living where there aren't any food crumbs or spills. The best cure—better than bug spray—is prevention. Open those cupboards and pull those drawers out; then reach way in with the dusting attachment of your vacuum cleaner and pick up all that stuff that insects like to munch on. Remove their food! It's a lot cheaper and safer than poisoning.

184 Worst first

Before you wash the kitchen ceiling vent or fan blades or filter in hot soapy water, take a paper towel and wipe off the bulk of that heavy, "furry" grease. Saves a mess!

185 Get it down

Those fan/motor units in kitchen ceiling vents that get coated with grease should be removed and cleaned on occasion. Take off the grill shield and unplug the fan; then lift and twist the unit a couple of inches on the mounts and out it will come, making it much easier and safer to clean.

186 Grease release

Kitchen filters take a long time collecting all that grease, and so they take a while to clean. Let the filter soak in a sinkful of hot dish detergent solution to loosen and dissolve the many layers of grease. Repeat with fresh solution as necessary.

187 Cut off at the pass

Grills, vents, and fans collect dust and, if never cleaned, will develop the "fur" that I spoke of. The secret of success is to put all grates, grills, and fans on a regular dusting schedule, whether you see dust on them or not, and the "fur" won't have a chance to build up. A lambswool duster is best for this purpose if you do the job often enough.

188 Washers: put the lid on it

The average house requires about five different types of faucet washers. I keep mine in a transparent plastic bottle with a lid, and shake it when I need to see and find the washer I want without dumping out the whole mess of them. The lid also helps keep them from getting dry and brittle before their time.

189 Royal flush

Garbage disposal repairmen tell me that disposal odor and the need for cleaning would be avoided if the user would just fill the sink half full of water before turning on the disposal, causing a large gush of water to hit the blades along with the garbage. The water washes and flushes the walls of the disposal. Running just a little water in with the garbage allows scraps of food to stick to the inside walls of the unit, where they will decay and stink. To get in shape for your royal flush campaign, try a packet of Ajax Disposal Cure. It beats ice cubes and orange peels hands down.

190 Trash compactor

The best compactor is a clean compactor. The best defense to keep it that way is not to confuse it with a garbage disposal for food waste. A compactor is mainly designed to handle dry trash. Organic waste will rot and smell. Save peelings and old produce for the composte heap. Keep out raw meat and fish and disposable diapers! In addition, remove compacted material often. Odors come from bacteria, and lots of bacteria can live in a compactor. Deodorant sprays might mask the smell, but removing the source of the smell is a better bet.

191 All's not in the bag

Clean garbage compactors when they're empty. Follow all pre-cleaning safety precautions in the owner's manual. Vacuum up all of the loose fallout. Then spray liberally with a disinfectant cleaner, wait five to six minutes, and scrub with a tank or long-handled brush. Wipe dry with a towel. Then give it a last shot of disinfectant, and leave it on to dry.

LADDERS

192 Just right

A five-foot stepladder is the best size to use around the house. Smaller ladders cause falls; bigger ones chip and nick the walls and woodwork.

193 Ladder leaning

Ladders always shift a little and, when they do, the bare metal can scratch or mark the wall. When I use an upright ladder, I always drape a terry cleaning cloth over each of the two legs that will rest against the wall.

194 Conditioning a ladder

Don't paint wooden ladders or planks that you use to stand on. The paint hides cracks and weaknesses in the wood. Instead, treat them with linseed oil when you're not going to use them for a while. Give the oil a chance to penetrate and dry.

195 Unsafe substitutes

Don't ever step, stand, lean, or sit on a shelf or a fireplace mantle to reach some nook to clean it. Often, shelves look strong but aren't. Sometimes they can peel right off and break you, them, and what's on them, too. The same goes for sinks in the bathroom; most are only anchored to the sheetrock well enough to hold their own weight, not yours!

196 Best angle

When you use an extension ladder, make sure it's set at a safe angle and firmly anchored to the ground. The base should be one foot out from the wall for every four feet of height. Never stand on the top rung.

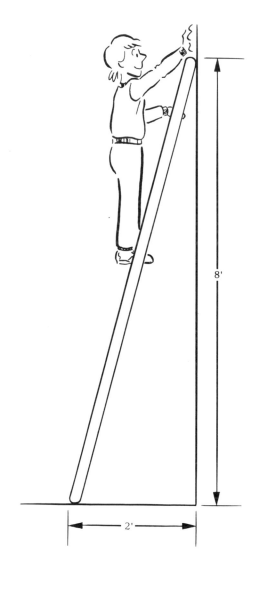

8'

2'

197 Ladder moving

Clear the ladder of buckets, pans, and tools before moving it. Save the surroundings and your nerves. A fall or spill is almost assured otherwise.

LAUNDRY

198 Did you know?

Cold rinse water not only saves energy, but it reduces wrinkles too!

199 The heat factor

Bleaches are the most effective in hot water, and they work slightly less effectively in warm water. Oxygen bleach hardly works at all in cold water. If you bleach, warm things up.

200 Wisk it away!

Dingy, yellowish laundry is the result of a longtime buildup of detergent and dirt residue in the fabric. Wisk Power Scoop concentrate contains a cleaning agent that reduces buildup with every use.

201 A laundry lesson

If you get a pink load from a dye transfer in the laundry, don't dry it! Instead, immediately rewash with a little bleach. It may take three to five washings, but most dye bleeding will come clean especially before the dye is set by heat drying.

202 Best to test

Before you use bleach on fabric, test it. Put a teaspoon of bleach in a quarter cup of water. Place a drop or two of this solution on a hidden section of the item to be bleached. Leave it a minute, and then blot with a white cloth. If you don't see any bleeding or color change in the fabric, it's okay to bleach.

203 Toss your lint mint!

Too much lint in the dryer will affect the dryer's efficiency, and worse, end up all over the floor where it can find its way into your mop water and floor wax. Wiping or vacuuming out the dryer filter on a regular basis is so easy it's worth remembering. Keep the dryer lint-free, and watch how much cleaner the whole house will be.

LIGHTS

204 More light

Light bulbs collect smoke, and that cuts the glow. Turn them off, let them cool down, and remove them. Wipe them down with a cloth dampened in all-purpose cleaner solution, then dry them well and replace them.

205 Long dirty lights

Fluorescent lights gradually get dirty and lose candle power; they last so long this is almost sure to happen, and when it does, we're always tempted to clean these fragile tubes in place—don't do it! You'll never get them clean this way. Do all the fluorescents in the house at once if you can. Twist them out to remove them and lay them on a damp towel on the counter. Then wipe them with a cloth that has been wet with all-purpose cleaner solution, and dry them with a soft cloth. Make sure they're good and dry before you put them back.

206 Handy is healthier

Don't fight your light fixtures. It's impossible to clean them properly while you're teetering on a chair, stepladder, or standing on the bed—stretched to your limit, swiping at them with a wet rag. Not one in one hundred can be cleaned well in place, and it's nice to survive the exploding bulb that wet cloth might create! Unscrew them and take the fixtures down; dump the bugs and wash removable glass parts in clean dishwater. Polish the parts dry and reassemble.

207 Get back on the fast track

Grimy track light tracks? Airborne dust and oils, attracted by the heat of the light, build up, unite, and cling hard, even to ceiling units. Track light tracks are generally coated with high-heat enamel paint, and they can be washed. Shut off the light and let it cool; then spray a cloth and wipe the track (not the light!) with all-purpose cleaner solution. Let the cleaner sit on there for a few minutes and then wipe the track good and dry.

208 Made in the shade

Ninety percent of fancy, flimsy lampshades can't really be cleaned. If they're stained or the light has faded them or cooked dirt onto them, forget it. If vacuuming, dry sponging, and gently spotting with dry cleaning fluid doesn't work, go shopping for new ones!

209 Lighten up

Clean fiberglass, plastic, and other washable types of lampshades by spraying all-purpose cleaner solution onto a cleaning cloth and wiping them down. Keep changing the cloth sides to avoid smearing.

210 Aerial attack

A crystal chandelier can be taken apart and washed a piece at a time. If reassembling it seems worse than solving Rubik's Cube, you can try spraying the crystals, just so long as you avoid spraying other parts. Use an ammonia solution and let it drip onto a thick pad of towels below. Keep spraying until the drops are clear. It will dry nicely by itself.

MASONRY

211 Seal, don't paint!

When a painted concrete floor gets a chip or two, the whole floor can look bad. Instead of paint, use a concrete sealer; it's tougher than wax, and you'll stop the dust from bleeding out of the concrete every time you sweep. A good coat of sealer keeps stains from penetrating and gives the floor a smooth finish that can be maintained easily. Even with a dust mop! You can buy concrete sealer at a janitorial supply or paint store.

212 A cement sponge

"Cinder block" is a cinch to clean if it has a good coat of block filler and two coats of paint on it. Bare masonry block is hard to clean and almost impossible to get stains out of, so paint it.

213 Outside walls

Pressure wash them. Pressure washers can be found in most rental places now. They're easy to use and will jar loose and wash away even embedded soil.

214 Paint pain

When paint drops and other stains on the surface of masonry refuse to budge in the face of chemicals, I sandpaper them off.

215 It's a hard fact!

Indoor brick is hard to damage but porous enough to absorb and hold oil, grease, handprints, food splatters, etc. You shouldn't use muriatic acid to clean brick; that's used only on newly laid brick to remove mortar, drips, etc. To clean indoor brick, vacuum first; next, dry sponge (see introduction);

then scrub with a strong detergent solution. Blot it immediately with a thick towel so that dirty water won't soak into the brick. The idea is to release the soil and then remove it right away.

216 Driveway spots

If your parking area is made of concrete, you can use almost any chemical or cleaner to clean oil stains from it, but if it's made of asphalt, the job isn't so simple. Solvents, such as paint thinner, gasoline, kerosene, or turpentine dissolve asphalt and cause it to deteriorate. The only safe remedy for stained asphalt is detergent cleaner.

217 A "hard" job

To clean soiled and stained concrete floors, use a strong solution of degreaser (available at a janitorial supply store). Flood the concrete with degreaser, let it sit for a few minutes, and then scrub it with a floor machine, black nylon pad, or nylon brush. Use a squeegee to gather the resulting muck into a puddle, pick it up with a dust pan, and dump it into a bucket. You might need to scrub and rinse it, too, if the concrete is filthy instead of just dirty.

218 The wet test

Concrete absorbs moisture when you clean it. Even after it looks dry, it is still releasing "sweat," and that's a bad time to wax, paint, or mop the concrete. If you're not sure whether the concrete is really dry, lay a rubber mat over it. If moisture doesn't accumulate under the mat after a few hours, it's okay to wax, paint, mop, or otherwise treat the concrete.

MATS

219 Mat stats

Eighty percent of the dirt in your home comes in on
foot through the doors. Place a good commercial
walkoff mat at each entry—both inside and out.
The rough exterior mat knocks off heavy mud and
gravel. The interior mat picks up fine soil and
moisture.

220 Ugly underfoot

Old familiar coco mats are out of date. They smell
like a dead dog when they're wet; they hold moisture; and the dirt never does come out completely
when you clean them. Nylon or olefin carpet-type
mats with rubber or vinyl backing are much better.

221 You'll regret wet

When you clean a rubber-backed mat, never put it back down wet. It will stay wet a long time underneath and can damage the floor and grow algae. Spray it with a hose and use a floor squeegee to remove the excess water; then hang it over a fence or railing until it's completely dry.

222 A sure fall!

Those "tire slice" link mats catch heels and trip up people. They don't stop much dirt, either. Get them out of your home and business before they get you.

223 Stick 'em down

Good door mats are important inside the door as well as out to keep dirt from being tracked in and tracked all over. How do you keep a mat from creeping on a carpeted floor? Get one of the special sticky underliners sold for just this purpose in mail order catalogs and hardware stores. Your mat will stay put and keep on cutting your housework time.

MISCELLANEOUS ITEMS

224 Aluminum alert

When cleaning aluminum cookware, don't use any cleaner that contains ammonia because it will pit the aluminum. Cream of tartar does a good job, and there are commercial cleaners made especially for aluminum.

225 Key cleaning

Computers do get dirty, not only from operator sweat, skin oil, makeup, and snacks, but as a result of their static attraction, which pulls dust and dirt on and into them. Dust them daily with a lintless Masslinn cloth. On a weekly basis, carefully vacuum the keyboard with the round brush attachment of a vacuum; professional computer cleaners hold the keyboard upside down and, with a soft toothbrush and a little bit of foam from your all-purpose cleaner solution, lightly scrub the outermost surface of the keyboard. This cuts even hand grease. Then wipe the keys to leave them clean and fresh. If you're not that brave, it's best to faithfully use a cover.

226 Subtle spraying

Never spray anything directly onto any part of a computer. Spray a cloth and then wipe with it, using nothing stronger than all-purpose cleaner solution.

227 Bogus bloomies

For the mind-boggling job of dusting artifical flower arrangements try a hair dryer set on cool and low.

228 Custom cleaning

There is an inexpensive adapter that fits your vacuum hose, and I recommend it for blowing and sucking a computer clean. It comes with three attachments: a mini crevice tool; an oval brush; and a round brush. They really get into the nooks and crannies of keyboards, typewriters, and stereo

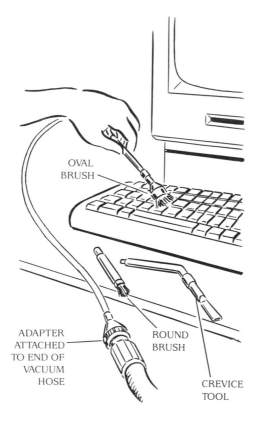

OVAL
BRUSH

ADAPTER
ATTACHED
TO END OF
VACUUM
HOSE

ROUND
BRUSH

CREVICE
TOOL

equipment. If you can't find this at a computer store, write to me at P.O. Box 39-J, Pocatello, ID 83204.

229 The gooseneck solution

To clean bottles with necks too small to get a dish cloth or bottle brush inside, fill the bottle halfway with dish cleaning solution and toss half a handful of rice inside. Shake like mad. It's amazing how fast and well this method cleans the inside.

230 High chair

High chairs get more food thrown on and over them than a garbage can. Dish soap diluted in a trigger-spray bottle is the best defense and offense. Spray it all over and let it sit a few minutes; polish dry with a terry towel.

231 More teeth to clean

Combs get pretty grungy, and wiping them or holding them under the tap won't do much to clean them. You need to soak dirty combs in dish detergent solution. The detergent will dissolve and release all the hair oil, hair spray, and even that super styling gel. Rinse and air dry.

232 Read 'em and wipe

Many paperback book covers are now laminated and can be damp-wiped safely. Go over the surface of the covers lightly with a cloth dampened in all-purpose cleaner solution, and wipe dry immediately. Be careful when cleaning book pages. With the exception of grease, which can be treated with K2R, and mud or other surface soil, which can sometimes be wiped off with a damp cloth, stains on paper are permanent, and trying to clean them may just make them worse.

233 Brighten your outlook

Hold your eyeglasses under a flowing tap to wash the unseen grit and dirt from the lens. While the glasses are still wet, take a drop of dish soap and rub the lens gently between your fingers. Massage the bridge, too, and other places where make-up, perspiration, and other particles may be caked on. Rinse well and dry with a soft cloth. This beats the old breathe-on-them-and-rub-with-your-shirttail routine.

234 Shabby shelving

Worn and porous inside cupboard surfaces are unsanitary and a pain to clean. If you're going to paint them, use a good hard enamel. If you live in an apartment or a rented home, pick up some of Rubbermaid's new vinyl shelf covering. It's inexpensive, rolls on in seconds, cleans like a breeze, and can be taken off easily when you leave (it cleans the surface when you pull it off, too!).

235 Dress up your drawers

Drawer fallout (that gradual build up of crumbs, lint, and bits and pieces of unknown things on the bottom of drawers) has to be dealt with. Drawers are cleaned fastest by emptying them, dumping the fallout, and then vacuuming the empty drawer. I always run a damp cloth over the inside of the drawer after that. Trying to vacuum the bottom of a drawer with everything still in it is an exercise in futility, and taking the vacuum apart to fish out a ring, bracelet, or small sock is a task no one likes.

236 The cedar cure

You can restore the moth-repelling aroma of cedar to a chest or closet by rubbing the surface with fine sandpaper. Be sure to go with the grain.

237 Unbind 'em

Fighting drawers that stick tears up them and you. Take a minute to find where the drawer is hitting the cabinet and simply sand it a little. Once the drawer works freely, rub some candle wax into the area that used to stick.

238 For a cleaner call

Telephones get grimy from hand and face oil. Spray disinfectant cleaner onto a cloth—not on or into the phone itself—and wipe the receiver down. Give the cleaner a minute or two to work on the grime; then buff dry. If you have teenagers, you'll probably need to clean the phone more often.

239 Cleaning artistry

Oil paintings get just as dirty as the walls but require a lot more delicacy when cleaning. We always dry sponge them with a rubber dry sponge (the one that looks like a giant eraser).

240 Getting the "knack" of it

Take knickknacks, figurines, and other washable small items to the kitchen sink for cleaning. Put a rubber mat in the bottom of the sink and lay those little treasures on a deep soft towel both before and after washing. You'll have less breakage, and the job will go faster.

241 A case for kid gloves

When it comes to cleaning art objects: think gentle! Three steps: (1) dust and vacuum first; (2) clean with a dry sponge (the rubber eraser-like sponge available at janitorial supply stores); (3) damp-wipe with a light solution of neutral cleaner, then dry immediately (avoid solvents, acids, and any kind of strong cleaner). If in doubt about how to clean it, take the item to an art expert.

242 Get the picture?

Pictures with glass fronts should never be cleaned by spraying cleaning solution directly on them or with a dripping rag or sponge. The solution will run down under the glass and absorb or leach up onto the paper or whatever is behind the glass. Spray the solution onto a cloth, and then damp-wipe the picture with the cloth, polishing dry immediately.

243 Mad at mildew?

Mildew is a live fungus growth, not dirt. Three things will combat it: (1) plenty of ventilation; (2) plenty of light; and (3) using disinfectant cleaner when you clean. Always allow the disinfectant solution to sit on the surface for 5 or 10 minutes to allow enough "kill" time before wiping. Then spray a light mist of solution on the clean area and let it dry. This will retard future growth.

244 Chapped chaps

If you have badly stained leather, take it to a pro! For just general cleanup and conditioning of any smooth (non-suede) leather, work up a lather of saddle soap and apply the foam generously to the item. Work it in well and it will work the dirt out. Use a white cloth so that you can see when the dirt stops coming off. When you reach that point, wipe off all the foam, and you're through.

245 Imitation leather?

Vinyl surfaces are pretty tough and forgiving, but keep solvents away when you're cleaning them. Use water-based cleaners, soft sponges, and cloths, and always rinse well when you're done to get rid of any potentially harmful residue.

246 Teddy bearable

After being dragged on the floor and drooled on a while, stuffed animals do need to be cleaned. The safest approach is to dampen a clean, white towel with a solution of Woolite or upholstery shampoo (you want more of the foam than the water) and gently rub it all over—just don't soak or overwet the critter. When your towel gets saturated with dirt, switch to a fresh one. When no more dirt comes out, give Teddy a rub rinse with the towel dampened in plain water. Then brush his fur back up so it won't dry with a cow lick. Let him air dry before you put him back in the petting zoo.

247 Careful with the camel!

Camel hair, angora, and all those expensive yarns used in fine clothing and furnishings are organic fibers just like wool and silk. This means you shouldn't use enzyme digesters on them; clean these special fibers with gentle soap like Woolite or a mild detergent, or dry clean.

248 Itch alert

Insulation material frequently contains fiberglass, which is made up of tiny (yes, glass!) fibers that will really itch once they get loose on you. Frequent vacuuming during any project involving fiberglass is the only reliable way to recover fiberglass particles.

249 Wicker quicker!

Food, drips, dust, bird droppings, airborne oils, etc. won't come off wicker with just plain water. You need a cleaner. Lightly sponge on some all-purpose cleaner solution to get the dirt off, but don't leave it on as long as you do when cleaning other surfaces. Flush or wipe with water to rinse, and then dry quickly with a thick towel. Wicker can only take so many wet cleanings before it collapses. Make those washings good ones.

250 A corker of a cleaner!

Clean corks with a dry sponge (the one that looks like a big rubber eraser).

251 Straw

Too much moisture ruins straw. Routinely vacuum or dust straw items. If they're visibly dirty, wipe them with a sponge or cloth dampened with a little detergent solution, but dry them quickly right after washing. Never immerse straw.

252 Surface saving

Don't use nail polish remover to take stains out of your cultured marble countertop or sink. It'll remove the spot and also a generous amount of the surface! Gently removing the stain with all-purpose cleaner solution and a white nylon scrub sponge may take a little more time, but at least it'll leave the surface looking like it's supposed to.

253 Metal

Many metals tend to oxidize and look dull. To polish them up, I use a product called Ouater (pronounced "water"). It's a cotton "rope" that's impregnated with metal polish and rolled up in a can. Just tear off an inch or two, and polish until the rope is black and the metal gleams. This polish leaves behind a slight protective coat of oil that retards future oxidation, and it's faster, cheaper, and less abrasive than other types of polish.

254 Chrome

Chrome is easy to clean if you do so with care. A light solution of all-purpose cleaner or alcohol-based cleaner such as Windex will clean it harmlessly. Don't leave any solution on chrome for any length of time; after cleaning chrome, promptly dry and polish it.

255 Stainless steel

Don't be surprised if you see stains or discolorations on stainless steel. Remember, it promised to be stain*less*, not non-staining, steel. It does stain, no matter what you do. Be wary of stainless steel "treatments"—they may make stainless steel look good for a while, but they sometimes become a stain and a pain themselves. The best way to clean stainless steel is with a white nylon scrub sponge and a little ammonia solution. This should keep stainless steel looking as good as new. To leave a finishing shine, rinse and buff dry with a terry cloth.

256 Aluminum

Always clean aluminum with its grain. Look closely; most aluminum has a slight pattern or flow line; follow it, and the aluminum will clean easier and look better.

257 Mirrors

Though there are a many different opinions on how to clean mirrors (newspaper is a popular material), mirrors are cleaned best and fastest with a spray bottle of alcohol-based window cleaner such as Windex and a dry lint-free cloth. Never spray a mirror directly, or it could run onto the edges and behind the mirror, causing the silver to oxidize, which creates annoying dull areas that can't be cleared away. Spray the solution onto a cloth, and then apply it to the mirror. Polish with a dry cloth until the mirror is free of streaks.

258 Classier glass

Believe it or not, glass, as smooth as it feels, has microscopic pores. That's why it fogs up. There are anti-fog products available for your windshields, mirrors, and even eyeglasses that make glass so slick it won't hold water. These products save time and trouble. When you apply the anti-fogger, water just slips off.

259 Clean the tar out of it

The nicotine and tar in smoking residue is what sticks to everything and is especially problematic on glass. Ammonia solution seems to cut it the best, and providing a good, strong circulation of outside air best removes the odor better than spray air fresheners.

260 Cleaning ashtrays

Ashtray tar and nicotine residue is sticky stuff. Clean ashtrays by dumping the contents, spraying two shots of all-purpose cleaner solution into them, and letting them sit for a while. Then when you come back the residue will have broken down and you can wipe with a dry terry cloth.

261 Grills and vents

The round brush attachment for the vacuum is great for grills and vents because it brushes them while pulling off the fuzzy stuff that tends to cling to vents. Dust on grills and vents is stuck on with grease build up. The dust has to be disturbed or it won't come off.

262 Garbage can cleaning

Maybe I'm getting lazy, but after dumping my plastic kitchen garbage container, I set it upside down over one of the lawn sprinklers for a few minutes instead of taking the time to scrub it out by hand. Goodbye stinky rancid residue. And sometimes I even jump into the sprinkler myself (only in the summer, of course)!

263 Let them breathe again

Too much dust build up is harmful to plants, but Mother Nature cleans them best. If you have to wash them, take a hose or hand spray bottle, or put them in the shower and flood them gently but generously. If they're really dusty and sticky, spray them first with a little diluted shampoo or ammonia solution and rinse well. Or, with delicate plants, put the solution on a paper towel first and wipe the leaves off gently. A *light* alkaline or ammonia solution actually makes a good fertilizer.

264 Clean camping

Don't dry clean your sleeping bag and then sleep in it without airing it out. Doing that could mean the end of the trail for you. Some dry cleaning solvents give off fumes that stay in the filling. Always wash sleeping bags if it's at all possible.

265 Getting a bang out of cleaning

To clean guns, pick up a gun-cleaning kit for a few dollars. It has all the tools, materials, and directions you'll need!

266 Two scoops please!

Fireplaces are hard to clean when they're filled to the brim with ashes, so clean them more often. Open the damper first so that fine airborne ash will be drawn up the chimney instead of out into the room. Then scoop the ashes into a metal bin with your trusty dust pan.

267 Blowtorch cleaning

When cleaning fireplaces, if there's even the slightest chance any live coals remain, don't even think of using your vacuum. The rapid air flow would convert your vacuum into the most effective flame thrower you've ever seen. Shovel the ash out first, and let it cool thoroughly before vacuuming.

268 Don't make soot soup!

Soot is scary if you attempt to clean it before vacuuming. Before cleaning sooty areas, always vacuum up any visible soot first. Permanent inks are made out of soot carbons. That ought to inspire you to carefully lift up all you can before you start applying any liquids.

269 Impress Santa

Chimneys do need to be cleaned. They collect a coating that, when accumulated, can ignite and become a literal blowtorch. You have two choices: hire an insured and experienced professional chimney sweep; or go to the hardware store and ask for chimney brushes and poles. They come with complete directions. Have fun.

MOPS

270 Mop choosing

Mop strings won't snag so often on chair legs, corners, and edges if the mop head is made of rayon and cotton instead of pure cotton. The rayon makes for a stronger string.

271 Handy handle

If you have the choice, a 54-inch handle on your sweeping, mopping, and other floor tools is much better in a house than a 60-inch handle. It will cut bumps and nicks about 50 percent.

272 Wiping, not watering

Whenever you see the instruction "damp mop," it means dip a mop in a bucket and then wring all possible moisture out before mopping. This will keep moisture out of cracks, and that's especially important for wood floors.

273 Nice extra tool

The best scrubber to arm yourself with when mopping a floor is a small, green nylon mesh pad. It will remove black marks, street tar, and hard soils.

274 Wringers are for wringing

Don't ever wring a mop with your bare hands!

Mops pick up glass, pins, needles, staples, thumb-tacks, toothpicks, and dozens of other sharp objects that can lacerate or puncture hands. Use a mop wringer or even step on the mop with your shoe if you have to, but never use your hands.

275 Beware of bleach

If your mop has gotten soiled and a little ugly, just rinse it twice after each use; don't bleach it. It may look cleaner after bleaching, but bleach will weaken the strands and make them snag off the next time you use the mop.

276 Mop care

If you feel your mop heads are getting unsightly, the washing machine's the place for them. Don't wash them loose, or they will tangle and frizz as if they were electrocuted. Put them in a mesh bag, then air dry them.

277 The right resting place

Always store a mop with the handle down and head up and turned out. It will dry without molding or stinking.

OUTDOOR

278 Hose versus broom

We've all been impressed with the cleanliness of

the Disney parks. They hose down their walks, driveways, and patios more often than they sweep them. If you have good water pressure and water is not scarce, try hosing such surfaces yourself. It's faster and more effective than any other cleaning method.

279 Squeegee away snow!

I do most of my light snow removal with a floor squeegee, one that looks like those at gas stations. It's fast and leaves the surface dryer.

280 Ice melt

An ice-melting chemical works best when it gets to a melted brine state, so leave the skim of water that will appear after you apply the chemical to surfaces.

281 Hot idea

The best way I've found to clean a barbecue grill is to wire brush it while it's hot. This knocks off charred grease globs and stuck-on food. The next barbecue fire will sanitize the grill.

282 Gas grill

After cleaning the inside of the gas grill, spray it with non-stick cooking spray. It will be a lot easier to clean next time.

283 Any season

To clean lawn furniture, I hit it right where it sits with a bucket full of all-purpose cleaner solution and a scrub brush. Flood the furniture and scrub it once to wet it down well, then scrub again to remove the loosened dirt. Now hose it down until the water that runs off is crystal clear and suds-free. Then knock or jar it a little to shake off loose water so that it won't get water spots.

284 Roll out the barrel

Garbage cans will always get that old familiar rancid smell and have to be washed. I scrape out the spills and stuck-on stuff, then (in the warmer months only) I spray the can well with the garden hose. Sometimes it all comes out, but if not, I pour a half-bucket of hot water and a squirt of dish detergent into the can, brush it all around, and let it sit for 10 minutes. Then I brush it again inside and out and dump the water into the yard (it won't hurt the shrubs or the driveway), rinse, and it's done.

285 Sparkling siding

That aluminum siding may be durable, but it isn't impervious to soil, sap, rain, mud, and bird bombs and can begin to look like it has been under attack. Have no fear. It can be washed using all-purpose cleaner solution. Spray or apply the solution as if you were washing a big car and let it sit for a few minutes. Then scrub the siding a little with an extended brush; next, hose it off. Don't worry about the plants or the lawn. A little phosphate or alkaline cleaner is actually good for them.

286 Pressure washing

Pressure washers can be rented inexpensively, or you might even want to own your own. They can dislodge deep-down dirt and stuck-on stuff and quickly clean large, hard-to-reach surfaces. Because a pressure washer only sprays water, I pre-spray with cleaning solution to loosen the dirt. Then I plug the washer in, point it, and put pressure on the soil until it surrenders!

287 Window wells

All right home owners, time to clean the litter-collecting area called the outside window wells. Get yourself a small bucket and put it down into the well; then by hand—a gloved hand, of course—pick up any leaves, pop cans, and other garbage you may find and put it in the bucket; then dump it all into a plastic bag. The bucket makes all the difference. (Trying to use a plastic bag alone creates a big mess and takes longer when the garbage blows back in the hole, as it tends to do.) My bucket method is so easy, you'll feel like cleaning your neighbor's well, too.

288 Clean plants

Mild solutions of dish detergent, ammonia, or other alkaline cleaners, when used to clean outdoors, won't hurt the lawn or shrubs. My friend Jerry Baker even uses such solutions to fertilize his plants and stimulate plant growth.

289 On-line cleaning

Whether made of wire or rope, clotheslines collect aerial fallout and transfer it to clothes placed on them. To prevent this, you need to keep the line clean. Soak a cloth in all-purpose cleaner solution and grip the line with it. Wipe gently, leaving enough solution behind to dissolve the dirt. Wait a minute, and then with a tight grip on the cloth, wipe the line again.

PAINT

290 Paint pointer

A top-of-the-line, brand-name paint (yes, that means higher priced) not only covers better and lasts longer but will often go much farther. It amazes me every time. Buy the best—it's cheaper in the long run!

291 That's a switch

The backside of a light switch plate is a handy place to keep a record of the color and type of paint you used for the room. When your ready to repaint, just screw it off.

292 Brush quality

Buy professional-quality brushes. Nylon bristles last and hold their "spring." An angled sash brush will improve your trimming accuracy.

293 Defeat those drips

Prevent paint-can drip! Punching a hole in the inside gutter of the can with a screwdriver or nail will eliminate "can run."

294 Roller lines

Ten seconds of trimming the fuzzy edges off a paint roller with a pair of scissors will help reduce those roller lines you always see after the paint dries.

295 Roller screen

Using one of those five-gallon plastic buckets with a roller screen set in it is the only way to roll on paint. Roller pans tip and spill, and paint dries too fast in them. Paint stores sell the screen, and sometimes it's possible to get the bucket free.

296 Overspray alert

Sprayers are becoming a more popular way to paint at home. Professional painters always rub Vaseline on their faces, necks, and other exposed skin before they start so that any overspray will wipe off easily when the job is done.

297 Pirate painting

Walking the plank is a safe way to paint. A simple ladder, plank, and sturdy wooden box make a great working platform.

298 Strainers

If you insist on using old hosiery for something (it makes a poor cleaning tool), use it for straining paint and then toss it away along with any undissolved paint curds.

299 Patching

When patching walls prior to painting, remember that any large holes and cracks need at least two applications of patching material because it shrinks when it dries. I always apply it so that it bulges out a little from the wall, allowing me to sand it after it dries.

300 Prime those patches!

If you patch before you paint, remember that patched spots absorb paint and tend to stand out. Always prime the patch before you do the actual painting.

301 Brush cleanup

The substance you use to clean a brush depends on whether the paint is water-based or oil-based. If it's oil-based, use paint thinner; otherwise use water. Let the brush soak a bit in a bucket of paint thinner or water. Agitate the brush up and down and around. Repeat until no traces of paint appear in the solvent. Then spin the brush dry by rolling the handle between the palms of your hands. To keep brushes soft, put a drop or two of cooking oil on them after cleaning and store them wrapped in aluminum foil or plastic.

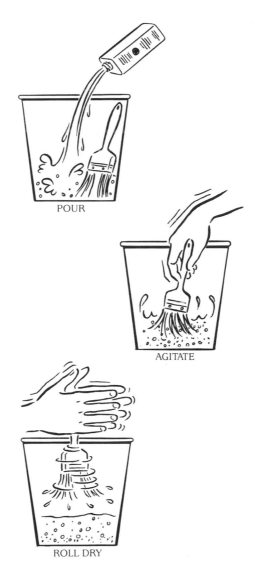

POUR

AGITATE

ROLL DRY

302 Roller cleanup

A roller can hold up to a cup of paint. Before cleaning a roller, always scrape it with the groove that you'll find in all paint stick handles. When you're finished cleaning the roller, always take it off the frame and let it dry. Never store a roller on the frame after cleaning. After you've pulled the roller from the frame, be sure to rinse the roller frame hubs. If you were to leave the roller on the frame, you'd ruin both the frame and the roller.

303 Right size

Too often we just grab a roll of masking tape off the shelf instead of buying it for the job at hand. Masking tape is available in ½-inch, ¾-inch, 1-inch, and larger widths. Don't buy tape wider than you need or so narrow that you have to double-tape.

304 Masking tape

Masking tape is easy to remove if taken off right after it's done its job. But the longer it sits, the tighter it sticks, and it may eventually be impossible to remove it without doing damage.

305 Masked mess

The minute you remove masking tape, roll it into a little ball, and wrap it in a piece of scrap paper. If you leave little wads of unwrapped tape around, or toss them in the trash basket, they'll stick to everything, including your shoes.

306 Masking tape residue

When all the stickum doesn't come off with the masking tape, the fastest and most modern way to remove it is to quickly dissolve it with a product called De-Solv-it. It helped clean up the oil slick in Alaska, and it makes short work of adhesive scum.

PETS

307 Hair

Vacuum suction alone just won't suck up all the hair—pet or human—that you'll find in your home. A beater-bar attachment for your canister vac or a beater bar on an upright is a must, especially if you have pets! Better yet, get your hands on a Pet Rake and you can remove hair easily from any type of surface, even tough ones like living room or car upholstery.

308 Give your cat a mat!

Giving a mat to the cat (or dog) is a very helpful preventative cleaning strategy. A rubber-backed nylon or olefin mat left in a pet's favorite hangout will provide a nice nesting place and collect pet messes that might otherwise end up all over the house. The mat is easy to vacuum or hose off and your pet will think you're the greatest.

309 Fleas

If fleas have taken over your house, all the vacuuming and scrubbing in the world won't get rid of them. Call an exterminator to fog the place; that's the only way you can infiltrate all of their favorite breeding grounds.

Flea Hideout Hotspot *Checklist

Many pet owners spend a lot of time and money trying to control fleas on their pets, yet they do nothing about the pets' environment. Yet fleas spend considerably more time off a pet than on it. They don't live on animals—they get a quick meal and jump down from the dinner table. At least 90 percent of their time is spent away from the host. As soon as fleas are killed on the pet, more jump on. For a flea-control program to be effective, you have to treat both the animal and his whole environment.

These are places fleas hide:

1. attic
2. under edges of throw rugs
3. lower part of draperies
4. beds
5. baseboards
6. walls to a height of about one foot
7. bird or rodent nests
8. shady areas outdoors
9. the inside of the car
10. bare dirt or sand
11. crawl space under house
12. vicinity of all entranceways
13. porch
14. grass or weeds
15. basement
16. carpeting
17. upholstered furniture
18. under furniture cushions
19. corners
20. edges of carpet
21. pet's bed and bedding
22. floor cracks
23. cracks and crevices (and other moist sheltered areas)
24. small holes that lead from outside to inside
25. hard floors
26. sandbox
27. windowsills

28. other favorite pet napping places indoors
29. doghouse and under doghouse
30. under outbuildings and sheds, and in the garage
31. favorite pet napping spots outdoors

*From *Pet Clean-up Made Easy*
© 1988 by Don A. Aslett

310 Pet stains

If your pet did "it" on an absorbent surface, such as carpet or upholstery, clean the spot with a bacteria/enzyme digester, a hungry little culture of helpful bacteria that you bring to life when you add warm water to it. The digester actually eats away the nasty organic matter that's causing the smell. Outright is the brand I use; follow the label directions and the smell will be out!

311 Spray

When cats spray, they generally do so in the same areas, over and over. A lot of the spray tends to seep down behind baseboards and into carpet padding where, if untreated, it will smell forever. If the spray is fresh, you might be able to get good results with a deodorizer/cleaner such as Nilodor, but if it's been there for more than a day, you'll need a bacteria/enzyme digester such as Outright to stop the odor. In either case, you need to apply enough cleaner to be sure it penetrates down as far as the spray did.

312 Urine

If you clean pet urine while it's fresh, it's no problem. Ordinary dish detergent will kill and clean away most of the bacteria and odors. If you let it go even for 24 hours, you'll get a permanent stain and longtime odor.

313 Number two

That most unpleasant pet poo is especially awful to contend with if you're trying to round it up with a piece of cardboard and a tissue. Keep an old six-inch squeegee and dust pan on hand for this duty, and once you've got it up, just flush your problem away. Then spray the area and cleaning tools with all-purpose cleaner solution and wipe dry.

314 Litter box bottom line

A standard 11x13-inch plastic dishpan with six-inch-high sides makes the best inexpensive litter box (sure beats a cardboard box). Savvy cat owners use an *un*slotted spoon when they clean out the box to pick up not only all the solid waste but those even more odoriferous "urine clumps."

315 Pet coloring

If your puppy's poop is leaving a reddish stain behind, change your brand of dog food. Many contain red food coloring to help them look like real meat. Don't be fooled; it doesn't fool Fido.

316 Tell by the smell

If you can tell by the smell that your home's previous owners had pets, you've got a tough job ahead of you. You can't just clean the carpets because some of the stain has seeped down into the padding. Pull back the carpet and replace the pad, at least in the soiled places (they'll be easy to spot). Then go after any stains around baseboards.

317 In the doghouse

Dogs do like clean houses, even if they do drag a few things in. First, dejunk the old bones and bits of beat-up stuff. If the doghouse has a floor, vacuum it, using the brush floor tool of your vacuum cleaner; then mist the whole inside lightly with disinfectant cleaner and let it dry. This will kill the germs that create odors and even discourage fleas.

PREVENTION

318 Simple saves

When you're building, remodeling, or redecorating, remember: the more kinds of materials and surfaces you have in a room or area, the more cleaning supplies and time it's going to take to clean it.

319 If in doubt check it out

If you're going to buy new tile, carpet, or other flooring, don't just think about style, pattern, and color; think about cleaning it for the next 15 or 20 years. When you see something you like, try to find someone who's lived with it for a while and how cleanable and durable it has proven to be. There's no better comparison shopping you could do.

320 Beware of buffet

To minimize party cleanup later, don't serve a buffet. When you have people walking around everywhere with overfilled paper plates, you're just asking for spills, stains, and scattered chicken bones.

321 Guest mess

Want to enjoy your guests more and spend less time cleaning up after they're gone? When they offer to help (wash dishes, make beds, sweep up), stop protesting and take them up on it. They'll enjoy their visit more, too.

322 Defeat dust

Good weather-sealing not only makes your house easier to heat and cool but also cuts down dusting dramatically.

323 Provide a place

It pays you back in time saved to have two or three extra waste containers around to put out when company arrives. More people make more garbage, and most people will pick up after themselves if there is an easy-to-find place for their trash.

324 Drastic plastic!

Don't store light and dark soft plastic items together. At the right temperature, the plasticizers in the plastic become "active" and will transfer color to, and stain, the lighter of the two. And this is one stain that can't be cleaned out or off.

325 Scotchgard

Soil retardants like Scotchgard are great for avoiding stains. They're often applied to carpet and upholstery, and even some clothing, right at the factory. Wear and repeated cleanings will remove it, but you or your dry cleaner or carpet cleaner can reapply it. If you do, be sure to follow the instructions on the container, and be sure that whatever you're treating has been cleaned first. I like to be sure the heavy traffic carpet areas, especially, remain treated.

326 Stain-proofed fabrics

Many people Scotchgard the bottom of their trouser cuffs, neckties, overcoats, baby bibs, the knees and elbows of kids clothes, the bottom of bed ruffles and curtains, fabric placemats and the seats of chairs. GOOD IDEA!

327 Vacation

If you want to return to a clean house, take these steps before you leave: (1) shut off the water; (2) flush the toilet; (3) don't leave fruit or food around; (4) take all garbage out; and (5) avoid leaving dirty laundry.

PROFESSIONAL HELP

328 Cleaning savvy from Uncle Sam

The government provides lots of homemaking help, some of it free. Write for a free Consumer Information Catalog, General Service Administration, P.O. Box 100, Pueblo, CO 81002.

329 Professional preliminaries

Getting outside help to clean? Great! Here are four ways to make sure you do it smoothly: (1) always check references; (2) get a firm price before they start—anyone who knows their business knows what it costs; (3) get a signed description of the job to be done; and (4) never pay in advance!

SAFETY

330 Storage

What goes up might come down—at the wrong time. Store heavy cleaning supplies down low. If they contain dangerous chemicals, make that low and locked.

331 Stairs

Don't store cleaning equipment on stairs—or even leave things there "temporarily." You might be programmed to dodge it, but visitors, the aged, and tiny ones are not, and stair falls are among the most dangerous.

332 Don't lose those labels

Labels on clothes are valuable but not nearly as valuable as the labels on chemicals. Never, never remove a cleaning solution label or transfer one cleaner into the container of another without relabeling. You may think you'll remember, but you won't. Whenever you fill an unmarked spray bottle, immediately take a permanent black marker and write on it what the bottle contains. It could save your furnishings or even your life.

333 Lifting

Lifting a full sack of garbage high out of the garbage can, can strain a back. To make the task more manageable, tilt the container over on its side and slide the sack out.

334 Sniffing can snuff

Some cleaners, finishes, solvents, and paints have fumes that, when inhaled—especially in a confined area—can be absorbed into your bloodstream and "intoxicate" you, setting you up for slips and falls. Always ventilate the room when cleaning.If it's winter time, wear a paper filter.

335 Save a kid!

Clean your shop area today! Put all sharp tools, glue, paint, and solvents out of reach. Unplug power tools. Get rid of any liquids or powders in unmarked containers.

336 Branding bucket

Don't ever set buckets or containers of cleaning solution onto furniture or wood floors. Even if the containers don't leak, they always end up with lots of little drips around them. And even if they just sit there, moisture can condense on the outside and cloud the wood's finish.

337 Oops!

While cleaning, always set buckets close to the walls rather than in the middle of the room or behind things. That will prevent you from "kicking the bucket" or tipping it over.

338 Electrical

Using soap and water to clean the outside of most electrical items is okay as long as you don't ever immerse them. Be sure to dry the item quickly and well. For these tasks, I use an all-purpose cleaner solution and a terry towel.

339 Broken glass

No matter how steady or callused your hand may be, sweep up sharp objects. Never pick up broken glass with your bare hands or a vacuum cleaner.

340 Shocking, but true

Water and watts don't mix. Always unplug anything and everything that you intend to clean.

341 Watch those sockets!

Don't flood cleaning solution over electrical receptacles, or that wall may be the last one you will ever have the chance to clean.

STAINS

342 Spot versus stain

What's the difference between a spot and a stain? A spot is *on*; a stain is *in*. If you catch a spot or stain when it's fresh, the chances for removal are 75 percent better. If the soiled item is washable, don't wait to wash it! Getting to a spot as quickly as possible keeps it from becoming a difficult or permanent stain. "Immediately" is the key word in successful stainbusting.

343 Pre-treat!

Pre-treating is the simple process of applying a chemical or cleaner to loosen or digest a spot or stain before you start the regular cleaning process. There are many good laundry pre-treats available, but if one is not at hand when you need it, make your own: rub a paste of enzyme detergent, or even your ordinary washday detergent, and a little water on the stubborn area. Let it sit on the garment for up to 30 minutes; then wash. Many a stain will be entirely removed by this simple procedure.

344 Blot!

Blot means *absorb*; as soon as a spill or spot is detected, hold a clean cloth tightly on it for a while and wait. Much of the moisture or grease will slowly transfer to the dry blotting cloth. A quick pat or rub doesn't allow enough time to "pull" the accident out.

345 Remove all you can first

Before you apply chemicals to a spot or stain, first blot up all the liquid and scrape up all the solid stain material you can. Work from the outside in, to prevent spreading the stain.

346 Bone scraper

If you need to remove a crusted stain and you don't have a professional bone scraper, a small plastic hand scraper or even a credit card will work.

347 Don't give the carpet an afro!

On carpet stains, especially, blot and don't scrub. If more treatment than that is called for, lay a towel on the spot and hit it with a brush to break up and absorb the residue. Scrubbing and rubbing will give your rug the frizzies and only make the spot more apparent—even if you do get the stain out.

348 Test

When using chemicals and solvents to remove stains, whenever possible test them in an inconspicuous area first to make sure damage or discoloration won't occur.

349 Stain surrender

When taking spots and stains out, always use white cloths. They'll tell you right away if the color is bleeding and if the spot is coming out.

350 Air dry— and why

Heat—especially from a dryer or iron—will "set" many stains, making them permanent. If you decide to try again later to remove a stubborn stain, be sure to keep the garment wet or air dry it.

351 Stain removal kit

Have a stain removing "arsenal" on hand: neutral detergent, such as liquid Dawn; common ammonia; dry spotter, such as Carbona or Energine; all-purpose spotter from a janitorial supply store; white vinegar; 3 percent hydrogen peroxide for bleaching; and a bacteria/enzyme digester, such as Outright.

352 Carpet spotting kit

You can make your own carpet spotting kit. Take a carryall or lunch pail and fill it with: carpet and upholstery shampoo for most water-soluble spots; dry spotter, for use on tar, grease, oil, ink, and similar spots; and a protein digestant such as Biz for removing blood, milk, chocolate, albumen, and other protein and food stains.

353 Watch those home remedies

Before you pull out home remedies such as peanut butter, margarine, or vegetable oil to try and remove a stain, realize that whatever you get out will be replaced by an oil stain from these food "removers," and that the oil stain can be harder to get out than the original spot. If your stain arsenal is depleted, the best home remedy is a hand dishwashing detergent, such as Dawn.

354 Fingernail polish remover

Fingernail polish remover will indeed dissolve almost anything—including many synthetic fabrics and carpets. Before you use it as a stain remover, be sure to test it first on a hidden spot and always use it carefully to avoid destructive spills.

355 Paint thinner

Paint thinner is one of the safest solvents to have around for home oil spills. It won't ignite easily, and it's almost odorless. Just blot it on oil or grease, and it will dissolve it.

356 That wicked wicking

To help prevent a carpet stain from "wicking," that is, reappearing because it has made its way back up to the surface from the roots of the carpet after you've removed it, place a ¾-inch-thick stack of clean dry towels over the spot, and weight the pile with a heavy object for about five hours. Any remaining stain will be sucked out of the carpet and into the cloth.

357 Stain removal aftercare

After using chemicals on a carpet stain, rinse! Then blot up as much moisture as possible with a terry towel. Remember that carpet pile has a "memory" and will dry in the direction it's left in when it's wet, so be sure to brush the nap to a standing position after the stain is gone.

358 Plugging

If you have a permanent stain in your carpet, such as aged urine, India ink, or bleach, you or a professional can plug it! Cut a circle of carpet out around the damaged spot; then cut one exactly the same size out of a saved scrap and make an exchange. You can glue or stitch the new clean spot in place. Brush the nap to hide the patch.

359 Hair spray

Yes, hair spray takes out some spots and stains, including ballpoint ink, because it contains either a lot of lacquer or alcohol, and both of these are great solvents. If you use hair spray to remove a stain, just remember to rinse the stain well afterward to get rid of the stuff that makes hair stiff.

360 Cleaning chemicals

A drop or two of most cleaning chemicals accidentally spilled on something won't do any harm, if you wipe it up and rinse the area well immediately. If you leave it, the water in the solution will evaporate, intensifying the strength of the solution, and the result will be a white, bleached spot.

361 Adhesive

To clean off the sticky glue from bygone bumper stickers, use a product called De-Solv-it. It softens and removes labels, adhesives, and gum. Blot and rub De-Solv-it on; don't pour it.

362 Chewing gum

Chewing gum globs got you down? Get some gum freeze at a janitorial supply store. This frigid spray, Freon, makes the gum brittle so that it will shatter and crumble. Make sure you vacuum up all the little crumbs before they turn soft again. Ice cubes will also work in the same way to remove gum.

363 Easter bunny blues

To remove chocolate spots from fabric, scrape off all you can with a dull knife; apply dry cleaning fluid; then follow with a coating of cool dish detergent solution of 20 parts water and 1 part dish detergent or all-purpose cleaner; blot; rinse; blot dry.

364 Dairy

To remove milk or ice cream from the carpet, apply ammonia solution or bacteria/enzyme digester; rinse. If the area is large, shampoo afterward.

365 Furniture polish

To remove furniture polish: apply dry cleaning fluid; blot; then apply a dish detergent solution made of

20 parts water and 1 part detergent; blot; rinse; blot dry. Don't be too optimistic; this stain is almost impossible to remove completely if you don't catch it while it's fresh.

366 Ink

To remove pen ink from fabric try the following in order: apply dry cleaning solvent and blot; then apply denatured alcohol; blot; apply nail polish remover if necessary, but don't use it on acetate fabric! If the stain remains, apply rust remover or oxalic acid solution. Professional plugging or bleaching may be necessary. Remember there are all kinds of inks, and they don't all come out the same way.

367 Grease and oil

To remove grease and oil from fabric: apply dry cleaning solvent, working toward the center to avoid a ring; blot; then apply detergent solution; rinse and blot.

368 Grass

If you can pre-treat a new grass stain with digestant, and then toss the stained item in the washer, you've hit upon the easiest way to deal with grass stains. If that's impossible, try the following stain removal procedure until the stain is gone: apply dish detergent solution; blot; rinse; blot again; then apply ammonia solution of 10 parts water to 1 part ammonia; blot; apply vinegar solution made up of equal parts white vinegar and water; blot; rinse; blot dry.

369 Grease spots on clothes

Oily spots on clothes after washing might be caused by a seal leak in the washer, but much more often they're caused by pouring liquid fabric softener directly into the wash, where it pockets. Always add softener to the dispenser or dilute it first in a quart of water and then pour it in. Fabric softener sheets may also cause spots in too hot a dryer.

370 Grease stains or spots

Oops, you notice a salad oil or grease stain on your suit, shirt, tie, or dress while you're eating. Hold a napkin against the spot; don't rub—just hold the napkin tightly against it to give the grease or oil a chance to transfer out of your clothes and into the more absorbent napkin. On ink, lipstick, or other marks, this technique has little or no value, but it removes most oil spots.

371 Snacker's smudge

Oily or greasy stains on paper—school reports, employment applications, or your living room wallpaper—are ugly and embarrassing. K2R, the aerosol solvent spotter, will remove them without a trace.

372 Jam or jelly stains

To remove jam or jelly from fabric try the following in order: apply all-purpose spotter or dish detergent solution diluted with 20 parts water; blot; apply vinegar solution of 2 parts water to 1 part white vinegar; blot; rinse; blot dry. If some "red" remains you might have to bleach the stain with 3 percent hydrogen peroxide.

373 Lipstick

To remove lipstick from fabrics try the following in order: scrape all you can off the surface, taking care not to spread the stain; apply dry cleaning fluid; blot; apply dish detergent solution with 20 parts water; blot; apply ammonia solution of 10 parts water to 1 part ammonia; blot; apply vinegar solution of equal parts white vinegar and water; blot; rinse; and blot. If a bit of stain remains, touch it with some bleach!

374 Mud

To remove mud from carpet: allow it to dry, and then brush or scrape off as much as possible; apply dish detergent solution of 20 parts water to 1 part dish detergent to what ever stain remains; blot; rinse; and blot dry. If the stain remains, apply a dry cleaning solvent; blot dry.

375 Mustard, ketchup

To remove mustard or ketchup: apply all-purpose spotter or dish detergent solution diluted with 20 parts water; blot. If the stain remains, apply rust remover or 3 percent hydrogen peroxide; blot. Do not use ammonia or alkaline cleaners. If a slight pinkish shade remains, a little bleach diluted with five parts water will remove it.

376 Mystery stain

If you don't know what a stain is, always try to remove it first with a dry cleaning fluid. If that doesn't cut it, then switch to water-based cleaners.

377 Just ask

If you come to a stain and don't know what it is, feel it and smell it, but your best bet would be to ask anyone who might possibly have made the stain to identify it. Dry cleaners say it is amazing that about 90 percent of the time, people can identify a stain when asked to do so. Try it at home!

378 Nail polish

To remove nail polish try the following in order: apply dry cleaning fluid; blot; apply nail polish remover after testing the fabric; then apply dish detergent diluted with 20 parts water; blot; apply white vinegar diluted with 2 parts water; blot; rinse; blot dry.

379 Latex paint

To remove fresh latex paint from carpet: soak with dish detergent diluted with 20 parts water; agitate; blot; rinse; blot. If the paint has dried, a little lacquer thinner will soften and remove it. (It could also melt certain kinds of carpet, so test first.) A Q-tip with a bit of paint remover touched on a hard drop of paint will also soften it back to its original liquid state so that it can be blotted and rinsed out.

380 Oil-based paint

To remove oil-based paint or varnish from carpet: check the label on the paint or varnish for the specific thinner or solvent to use. If the spot is already dry, soften it by covering it for several hours with towels dampened with the appropriate solvent; agitate with a brush, repeat as necessary; apply detergent solution and work into the stain; blot; rinse with warm water; blot dry.

381 Pitch

Pine pitch can be stubborn, and it can make you smell like the forest primeval. Turpentine, made from pine tree derivatives, takes it out and off!

382 Post-birthday blues

Wax drips on your tablecloth or carpet? You're in luck if you have an iron. Just set a clean absorbent cloth over the wax and hold a hot iron on it. The iron will melt the wax and the wax will pull up into the cloth. Any stain that remains can then be blotted out with dry cleaning fluid.

383 Rust

Rust (iron oxide) usually comes out best with professional rust remover, which is easily available at janitorial supply stores. Follow the instructions—especially the safety precautions. If you're determined to use or must use a home remedy, saturate the spot in lemon juice, dry it in the sun, and repeat until it's gone!

384 Shoe polish

To remove shoe polish from carpet: apply dry cleaning fluid and blot; apply dish detergent diluted with 20 parts water; blot; apply ammonia diluted with 10 parts water; blot; rinse; blot dry. If the stain remains, it may be necessary to bleach it with 3 percent hydrogen peroxide or plug it with extra carpet.

385 Red

It's a struggle to get "red" out of anything. Red stains, such as those from red wine, Kool-Aid, and berries, are the worst. No wonder we pros have a saying, "If it's red, you're dead." In the past, when this stubborn hue was left behind, bleach or scissors were the last resorts. Now there is a chemical available called Red Out. It removes stain by heat transfer. You apply the solution and place a wet, white cotton cloth over the stain. Then you hold a steam iron, set on high, over it for 20 to 30 seconds and repeat until the stain is gone. Complete instructions come with Red Out, and you can find it at janitorial supply stores.

386 Tar

To remove tar, scrape up all you can. If it's dry and hard, freeze with dry ice or gum freeze from a janitorial supply store, then shatter. Apply dry cleaning fluid or paint thinner to the remaining residue and blot with a thirsty cloth; repeat as necessary as it will take time to pull out all the tar residue. Next, apply dish detergent diluted with 20 parts water; blot; rinse; and blot dry.

387 Soft drinks

To remove soft drink stains from carpet: after blotting up all you can, apply all-purpose spotter or dish detergent diluted with 20 parts water; blot; rinse and blot. Aged red soft drink stains might be permanent or call for a little bleaching.

388 Urine

If a urine stain doesn't come out in the wash—stop! Don't toss the stained item in the dryer; heat will only set the stain. Pre-treat the stain with Wisk or a thick paste of Biz and water; let it sit for 30 minutes and then run the item through the washer again. You'll be surprised how often it all comes out the second time around.

389 Vomit on hard surfaces

Vomit is made of acid and protein, and so an alkaline cleaner, such as detergent—even dish detergent—will do a lot to neutralize and remove it. Here's another opportunity to use the old six-inch squeegee and dustpan and make light work of a yucky situation.

390 Vomit on soft surfaces

To remove vomit from carpet and other absorbent surfaces, scrape up as much as possible, and then rinse the spot well with water. Apply a bacteria/enzyme digester, such as Outright, according to directions. Be sure to keep the spot wet and warm for a while so that the bacteria can consume all that smelly stuff.

TILES

391 Tile truths

The dozens of types of tiles available—stone, brick, ceramic, and quarry tile—make it difficult to recommend a single method for cleaning them. Ask the dealer (or someone at your local janitorial supply store) for a penetrating seal appropriate for your kind of tile. This will give the tile a base on which you can then apply a wax or acrylic finish to make them shine and to make them easier to clean. Remember that tiles intended to have a highly textured or rustic look will never shine, no matter what—so don't waste your time and energy. Talk to your dealer if you're not sure of your options.

392 Go for the glow!

The reason for those streaks on ceramic tile is soap or water residue left behind. After cleaning tiles, wipe and polish them with a clean dry cloth; the surface will again shine, reflecting light instead of absorbing it.

393 Grout stains out

Grout is masonry, which means it's porous, and if left unsealed it will stain and be ugly. If this happens, you need to clean it well with a tough degreaser. A good scrubbing and rinsing, and maybe even a slight bleaching, is necessary to get it back to its original beauty. Then go to a Color Tile Store or masonry dealer and get a good penetrating seal. Use this to seal your grout joints just as you did your tiles. Follow the directions carefully. Now dirt can't soak in anymore!

TOOLS

394 The scrub pad spectrum

Nylon scrubbing pads and sponges are generally coded by color. The darker the pad, the more aggressive it usually is. White nylon pads are the safest and softest, and it goes uphill from there.

395 My favorite cleaning tool

The white nylon-backed scrub sponge is the key to safe scrubbing and scouring. Wet, it has just enough abrasion to dislodge stubborn clinging soils without hurting the surface underneath, and so it's safe to use on almost everything. Then flip it over, the sponge side will absorb the mess and wipe it away.

396 Rag versus sponge

For applying cleaning solution, a sponge is far better than a rag; it holds more solution and distributes it more evenly and quickly. You can pick up liquid spills with it faster, too.

397 Cleaning cloth heaven

Pro secret #1: How to make your own unbeatable cleaning cloths out of old terry bath towels. Cut an 18x18-inch square of heavy terry cloth and hem all the edges. Fold it over and stitch together on the long side. It will be hollow like a tube. Fold once—then again—and it will just fit your hand. By changing sides, and turning it inside out, you have sixteen sides to clean with.

398 Paper towels

Paper towels are great to use for chores that can be disgusting, like cleaning the top of the fridge, wiping up the first coat of oven cleaner, or disposing of doggie-doo-doo. But for most cleaning, use a terry cleaning cloth that can be laundered and reused.

399 Dry sponge

A dry sponge is great for cleaning wallpaper, acoustical tile, oil paintings, and smoke or soot—any surface where water would be a problem. A dry sponge also works well on masonry and most flat-painted walls and ceilings. It works like a giant eraser.

400 Those wretched "rags"

The best cleaning cloths suck up water and absorb. Don't try to salvage those old leisure suits or anything made of synthetics by turning them into cleaning rags—they just won't do any good. Polyester hates water, so how could it clean?

401 No more soggy sponges

Even if you keep your cleaning supplies in several locations, as I recommend, you should designate one central area your main cleaning station and house larger tools, vacuums, and extra cleaning supplies there. Be sure it's well ventilated so that all of those wet, soggy things will have a chance to dry properly. Hang up everything that can be hung—brooms, mops, and dust mops—and use wire baskets for the rest.

402 Brush crush

The best scrub brush is one with nylon bristles. It cleans and sanitizes well and has plenty of scrub power. Choose the style called "utility" or "tank brush." These are sold at janitorial supply stores. They have handles that will protect your hands and knuckles from scrapes, crud, and chemicals.

403 Steel wool woes

I know some of you still use steel wool to clean with (I've switched to nylon pads). The minute you finish using a piece of steel wool, dispose of it. If you toss it in the drawer or set it in the sink it'll rust and stain up the drawer or the drainboard, short out an old eight-volt battery, ignite (yes, steel wool will really catch fire) and burn down your house or apartment.

404 Tools at your fingertips

It makes sense to keep cleaning supplies as close as possible to where you use them. If you have to go to the basement or dig through a cluttered sink cupboard to find them, you're likely to lose your ambition to clean. Plastic caddies make it easy to assemble kits of supplies in each bathroom and every place you clean frequently.

405 Caddy

Pros use janitor or maid carts with wheels that are impractical for a home. A miniature version, however, is available. The cleaning caddy—a plastic tool tote with pockets and compartments to keep things neat—has a handle that makes it easy to grab and carry everything you need with you. Keep each cleaning station equipped with one.

406 Cleaning your cleaning cloths

Cleaning cloths can be used over and over, but they have to be kept supple! Always launder them just like clothes and dry them in the dryer, never on the clothesline.

407 Glove love

I keep partially used motel bottles of hand lotion in my work areas and heavily lotion my hands before I put on my leather work gloves. This keeps the gloves soft inside, and when I have to do hard cleaning with my hands, my gloves serve as a first aid station for them.

408 Helping hands

Hands are delicate and need all the help they can get. Before starting those extra messy jobs, rub a little liquid hand soap into your hands, and let it dry. The soap acts as a protective covering and repels dirt, which means less scrubbing. Then when it comes time to wash up just stick your hands under the faucet. Grubby nails, stained cuticles, and rough red hands will be a thing of the past.

409 Apron

A cleaning apron can save time when you've got a lot of nonstop cleaning to do. Besides protecting your clothes, the pockets keep all the things you need close at hand. On the other hand, if you were to use every wasted minute of your life to clean (like during commercials or while you're waiting for the pot to boil), you'd never need to do any non-stop cleaning.

410 Broom owners beware

To keep your broom like new, hang it up! Standing a broom on its bristles causes it to curl. (That may be okay if you like to stand at an angle while you sweep.)

411 More broom care

Brooms do get dirty. Occasionally dip about a third of the brush into fresh mop water and slosh it around a bit; then rinse and shake the water off. That will clean your brooms and make them clean better!

412 Handles

I've put bicycle grips on the end of mops and brooms for better grip and to keep them from marking when they lean or fall against things. You can buy them at bike shops, of course, and at some hardware stores.

413 Dust pan

My favorite way to use a dust pan is not to pick up dust and swept-up dirt but to pick up liquid. For this purpose a metal one will never do; you need a rubber dust pan. It won't get bent, and so it will keep its shape better, be more flexible, and butt right up to the surface of the floor even if the surface is a shade irregular. A dust pan is much easier and cleaner to use for large spills than a sponge. Best of all, a rubber dust pan won't rust!

414 Two-compartment bucket

Save your money when buying a bucket. Two-compartment buckets made for cleaning may look clever, but they will drive you crazy when you try to empty one side without spilling the other. A square bucket or a ten-quart Rubbermaid Roughneck is my favorite for household use.

415 Angle broom

If you don't already have one, go get yourself an angle broom. The split-tipped bristles catch even the finest dust, and this is one broom that's actually designed to match your natural broom stroke. It reaches into corners better, too.

416 Five-minute floor scrubber

Another professional cleaning tool is the Doodlebug or Scrubbee Doo, which is actually seven tools in one. With it you can scrub floors or shower walls quickly and effortlessly, and with just a switch of the interchangeable heads you can dust mop, apply wax, and even clean concrete. The swivel-action head means you never have to get on your hands and knees again. You can get one at a janitorial supply store.

417 Floor squeegee

After you scrub the floor and have accumulated lots of dirty, soapy water on it, don't mop it up; that takes too long and you'll have to change the water many times: instead, use a squeegee to push it into a puddle, and pick it up quickly with a dust pan. This will get rid of the mess fast. Then, just lightly damp mop and you'll be ready to apply wax or finish.

418 Foot loose and fancy free

I once heard someone suggest sewing a scrub brush onto old house slippers. Don't be persuaded to wear cleaning tools on your feet. Such a stunt might have gotten a laugh for Charlie Chaplin but, in general, attaching cleaning supplies to your person doesn't make cleaning fast or easy; it's an accident waiting to happen.

VACUUM

419 Pro power

Go down to your janitorial supply store and get a *commercial* upright vacuum. It's a rugged machine that you can really depend on. They have stronger motors, more suction, and longer cords, they're more maneuverable and cover more ground faster. Replacement parts are readily available, too.

420 Wider is wiser

If you have a big house and lots of carpet, use one of those new wide-track vacuums such as the one Eureka makes. It covers a 16-inch swath of carpet at a time, instead of the usual 10 or 12, and it will shorten your vacuuming time by at least a third.

421 Sweepers just sweep

Carpet sweepers are handy and okay for surface litter, like dropped popcorn, but they don't pull out embedded dirt. The carpet may appear clean, but it will soon fill up with dirt. Don't use a sweeper instead of a vacuum on a regular basis.

422 How to vac

When vacuuming, one leisurely stroke will beat five short swipes any day. Take your time and let the vacuum work for you. It needs time for the beater bar to loosen the dirt and for the air flow to suck it up.

423 Getting the edge

Dirt on wall-to-wall carpet edges isn't likely to be ground in underfoot, resulting in fiber damage and deterioration, and so don't worry about the edges unless they look bad. Occasionally, before you start vacuuming take a broom and flick the dust and debris out where the vacuum will get to it. This will save lots of vacuuming time.

424 Vacuuming stairs

Vacuum the center traffic areas of carpeted stairs with your beater bar vacuum to get out that ground in and embedded dirt. You can just wipe the sides, which are hardly ever stepped on, with a damp cloth, or dust them off quickly with a broom. Concentrate your energy where it's really needed.

425 Fringe frenzies

Those decorative fringes on area rugs will always collect dirt, lint, and dust bunnies. They're a nightmare to vacuum but not to hand brush. Just brush them with a shop or counter brush using a down and away stroke. This will whisk out the soil so that you can just sweep or vacuum it, and not the fringes, up.

426 Leaking dust

If you smell something when you start up the vacuum, it's resident dust, and it's escaping from your vacuum. Check the snap, zipper, or seal on your vacuum bag to see what's loose.

427 Indisposed?

Don't even think about reusing a disposable paper vacuum bag to save money. It'll probably get ripped in the process of trying to empty and reinstall it, and you'll spill dirt, dust, and dead flies everywhere. Even if that doesn't happen, the pores in the paper walls of the bag are already filled and clogged with dust because trapping dust is what they're designed to do. Reusing a bag would cut down considerably on your vacuum's effectiveness.

428 Bag basics

Once your vacuum bag is more than a quarter full, it loses half its suction power. Stop making double passes trying to get the carpet clean; empty or replace your bag and get it with the first pass.

429 Plugged

Is your vacuum cleaner losing suction? The culprit is most likely a plugged vacuum hose. Items such as toothpicks and broomstraws can lodge crossways in the hose and then snag other items that get sucked in, cutting off the flow of air. First try reversing the hose for a minute to see if you can push the clog out. If that doesn't do the trick, a mop handle, dowel, or even a small garden hose should work to dislodge the clog.

430 Metal alert

Vacuuming up small metal objects on the floor will damage vacuums eventually, if not immediately. We pros avoid this by mounting a small, strong magnet on the vacuum head. All those stray nuts and bolts, paper clips, and bobby pins will jump right up on there and stick so that you can remove them later. You can get such a magnet at your janitorial supply store; my favorite one comes from VacuMag, 6053 Corporal Lane, Boise, ID 83704.

 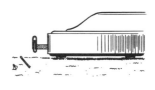

431 Fan

Every time you suck up a BB or a marble, it takes a chip out of the fan inside that creates the suction. Take pity on your faithful vac. Pick up the big obstacles by hand before you turn the machine on. Reduced suction can double your vacuuming time. A repair shop can replace a damaged fan for a nominal charge.

432 Beater bar safety

Don't risk your fingertips! Never reach under a vacuum with a beater bar to see if the beater is working. Instead, lift the vacuum up and look. The beater on a vacuum should rotate clockwise so that it brushes dirt into the path of the suction. If you put the belt on backwards, it will often reverse the beater and kick the dirt away from you. Look but don't feel underneath to see if it's going in the right direction.

433 Beware of backward belts

The beater on a vacuum should rotate clockwise so that it brushes dirt into the path of the suction. If you put the belt on backwards, it will often reverse the beater and kick the dirt away from you. Look but don't feel underneath to see if it's going in the right direction.

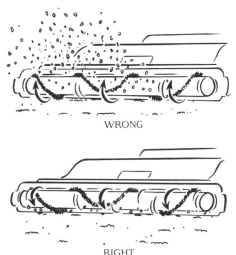

WRONG

RIGHT

434 Pile adjustment

Setting your vacuum, if possible, to the right pile adjustment is important. This gives the vacuum room to move to loosen deep dirt and assures that the suction will be able to carry the debris into the bag. Set the brush to its highest setting, which will bring it high up off the floor. Lower the brush gradually until you hear it lightly come in contact with the carpet—that's the setting you want. If you set it too low, you cut off the air flow and slow down the beater bar.

435 Belt-breaking work

Keep breaking vacuum belts? Stop trying to vacuum up overshoes and TV knobs! If that's not the problem, it may be that the belt isn't the right size. When belts don't fit, they slip at very high speeds. Make sure the belts you buy are intended for your model.

436 Better belts

Buy good vacuum belts instead of cheap ones. If they haven't broken in a year, replace them anyway so they don't start slipping. Your vacuum will run a lot better.

437 Cut the cord!

Eureka has a medium-duty cordless upright vacuum now that weighs about 10 pounds; it's called Freedom. For such quiet and convenience it's relatively inexpensive. I particularly recommend it for small apartments.

438 Double up

Two-story houses should be two-vacuum houses. Each vacuum will last twice as long, and so you'll come out even in the end. In fact, the beating you, the vacuum, and the stairs take when you are endlessly transporting the vacuum up and down between floors ends up costing you much, much more in wear and tear, and in energy.

439 Hand-held

Those little hand-held vacuums looked worthless to me at first, but for certain purposes you can't beat the convenience. Mount them any place you need to pick up a little...a lot of times a week. I have four of them at home now!

440 Book 'em

Your vacuum's round brush attachment is perfect for keeping books neat. Hold the book by the spine and quickly vacuum around all the edges.

VEHICLES

441 Dusty dashboards

Carry a New Pig dustcloth, a new type of cloth with built-in electrostatic action, from Dupont, in your glove compartment. It picks up and holds dust like a magnet. It can dust the dash, door—anywhere—anytime you're idle. Launder the cloth when it's saturated and reuse it up to 100 times. One inexpensive New Pig will outlast three cars.

442 Your own car wash

Here's my favorite do-it-yourself method for washing the car: get the hose running; spray the auto all over well; and then work it over with a bucket of all-purpose cleaner solution and the auto brush; rinse immediately and well. An auto brush is the best tool for spiffing up wheels, spokes, and grilles. Never wash your car in direct sunlight.

443 For finer fabric

Some of us "live" in our cars, and eventually it looks like it. Car upholstery can be shampooed just like a couch or carpet, but you'll need to rent a hand extractor. Vacuum the upholstery well. Then pre-spray any stained or soiled spots. Apply the shampoo all over, then extract it! I wouldn't worry about cleaning the ceiling upholstery unless the driver is over seven feet tall and rubs his head on it.

444 Unstick the ickies

Paint thinner removes rubber mastic glue that car makers use to attach rubber trim to car trunks and doors. It's that sticky stuff that comes off on your hands and luggage when you load and unload.

445 Contain it!

I've heard that some bosses, before hiring you, look in the trunk of your car to get a peek at your personal neatness. I finally began using a small duffle bag to store my jumper cables, gloves, etc. I've not had to dejunk my trunk since!

446 Clean trip

Carry a polypropylene (artificial turf) mat in your RV or trailer. Toss it out on the ground when you leave, and step onto it on your way back. Saves many post-camping cleaning hours.

WALLS AND CEILINGS

447 Baseboards

Before you wash a wall, take a damp cloth and wipe down the baseboard. This will pick up handfuls of hair, dust, and debris that would otherwise get on your sponge and be distributed all over the wall during cleaning

448 Vinyl wall covering

To clean vinyl walls, don't use harsh or abrasive cleaners. Use a mild neutral detergent, keeping the sponge nearly dry. Don't soak the seams. After damp-wiping, dry thoroughly with a cleaning cloth.

449 Textured wall coverings

Any textured wall covering such as burlap will have dust and dirt resting in the thousands of little pockets of the design, which will spread out all over when the wall is wet or rubbed. Always vacuum walls like these first before wet or dry cleaning. Trust me, even if you can't see it, it's there!

450 Two-bucket technique

My two-bucket technique is great for washing walls. Start with one bucket half full of cleaning solution and one empty bucket. Use a sponge soaked in the cleaning solution to go over the area to be cleaned, and give the solution a couple of minutes to work the dirt loose. Go back over the area again to pick up the dirty solution, and squeeze the sponge out into the empty bucket. When you're done, your cleaning water will still be crystal clear and the other bucket will be holding all the muck.

451 Sheetrock

Sheetrock is a paper-covered gypsum product. If it's dirty, paint it. You don't ever want to get water on raw, unfinished sheetrock.

452 Take it from the top

Always clean walls from the top down. Years ago, when we used calcimine paint and lye soaps, dribbles "burned" dirt marks into the walls, and so people learned to clean from the bottom up. Not any more! Clean your walls from the top down!

453 Black marks

Dissolve black marks on the wall from kids' chairs, cleaning tools, etc., don't scrub them. Spray the spots with all-purpose cleaner solution, and then gently coax them off with a white nylon scrub sponge.

454 Wallpaper

To clean old-style (non-vinyl) wallpaper, use a dry sponge, that is, a rubber sponge available at janitorial supply stores, which works like a giant eraser. Clean with the flow of the design. If you have vinyl wall covering, you can remove spots and smudges with a damp sponge.

455 Wall shepherding

If you run into velvet or flocked wall covering, be careful! Use a dry sponge on it, and use dry spotter to remove grease stains.

456 Wallpaper removal

I have my old wallpaper removed professionally because sometimes it's six layers deep. When I first tried to do it myself, I struggled with every method, from machines to matches. If you insist on doing the job yourself, this is the method I recommend: Using a big cellulose sponge and buckets of the hottest water possible, wet the surface down again and again and again. Keep the paper wet; this will get boring, but keep going. Eventually the paper will begin to bubble. Resist the temptation to pick at or peel the bubbles; keep wetting. The bubbles will get bigger and more tempting; not yet, keep wetting. Finally the whole sheet will come loose; now you can peel! Surprisingly, most of the old glue and paste will come off too. Just have patience, and the job will be easier, faster, and less messy than with any other method.

457 Nail and stud line dirt

Nail and stud line dirt on your wall is generally caused by poor insulation, not poor housekeeping. It can be cleaned off, but use enamel paint next time for easier washing.

458 Painting baseboards

Most baseboards have been accidentally waxed

many times. Before they can be repainted, the wax has to come off. Scrub the baseboard with ammonia solution; then lightly sand it so the new paint, which is really going to take a licking, will stick.

459 Acoustical ceilings

If you have acoustical ceilings, clean them with a rubber dry sponge. If they're too dirty for that or entirely beyond cleaning, repaint them with a very light coat of latex, not enamel, paint, which will allow them to retain at least some of their sound absorbent quality. If a stain bleeds through the latex, brush on a bit of clear shellac to seal the stain, and then let it dry and paint over it.

460 Textured ceilings

Don't wash unpainted textured ceilings. They may look like cement or plaster, but when wet they may dissolve and turn gooey. Dry sponge them; then paint to give the surface a protective sealing coat.

461 Stalactite

If the ceiling's texture is too sharp-toothed to clean, run a board lightly over the surface to knock the extreme points off; then give the whole ceiling a couple of heavy coats of enamel paint. Even deep texture can be cleaned after that.

462 Exposed beams

To dust exposed beams, use a lambswool duster on an extension handle. Hit both the sides and the bottom of the beams to loosen any cobwebs. Beams look better rugged, and so don't worry about washing them for many years.

463 Wash it, don't oil it

Too much furniture polish and too many oil treatments on paneling will make it sticky, attracting dust and dirt. A better option is to wash it with a mild oil soap solution and polish it dry with a terry cleaning cloth; that will leave the surface clean and give it a nice, low-luster sheen.

464 Wood paneling

That handsome grain on wood paneling can conceal a lot of soil. If it's coated with varnish or polyurethane, you can wash it. I clean paneling like this with a mild solution of oil soap (such as Murphy's Oil Soap). Squeeze the sponge almost dry and sponge the solution on; then wring out the dirty sponge into an empty bucket, not into your cleaning solution. Buff the paneling dry with a terry cleaning cloth.

465 Grain gain

When you clean paneling, or any wood, always rub it dry with the grain. When you do that, even bad streaks won't show!

466 Synthetic wood paneling

Much paneling these days is synthetic, that is, fake wood that often consists of wood grain photo reproduced onto composition board. You can wash it like other paneling, but be especially careful not to leave moisture on for very long.

467 Unfinished paneling

To clean unfinished paneling, remember that bare wood absorbs everything and stains easily. Vacuum the paneling first with a dust brush attachment; then dry clean with a rubber dry sponge, wiping with the grain. Use water only as necessary—and cautiously—to blot and remove marks. Avoid using cleansers of any kind. If you clean often you will need less water and avoid stains.

468 Refinishing wood paneling

If paneling is old, nicked, and tired, and you want to resurrect it, first clean it brutally with ammonia solution or a good strong solution of heavy-duty cleaner to get off all the old dirt and polish. I promise that if you aren't thorough, the new coat of varnish won't stick. After cleaning, touch it up as needed with fine sandpaper, working with the grain of the wood. Then restain the chips and nicks and sanded spots as necessary, making sure the color blends well. Now apply a coat of satin-finish polyurethane or varnish. You'll be surprised how much of a difference this kind of clean and repair job can make.

469 Choosing paneling

When choosing paneling for cleanability, avoid extremely dark colors—they show dust like crazy. Rich, mid-tone wood grain hides a multitude of cleaning sins.

WINDOW AREAS

470 Hang it!

A simple coat hanger will protect drapes from damage during carpet cleaning or other jobs in the vicinity. Fold the drapes in half like pants or slacks over the hanger, and place the hanger on the curtain rod.

471 Curtains

You may have heard that you can toss unwashable curtains into the dryer to clean them. The tumbling and air circulation is supposed to loosen and suck soils away, but I don't recommend the practice. It is not a cure-all. If you do it: (1) be sure the dryer is on "air," not hot; and (2) never use this treatment on sun-rotted drapes that will disintegrate, or plastic fabrics that might melt, or fiberglass. Your clothes will have fiberglass slivers in them for the next 20 years or for the greatly reduced life of the dryer!

472 Dust duty

Dust will come off all blinds easily, even mini-blinds, if you dust them *often*! If the dust is left on, it blends with sticky airborne oils and becomes a stubborn sticky coating that requires much more time-consuming cleaning. Dust often, using a lamb-swool puff duster on closed blinds.

473 Screens

Screens become embedded with bugs, dirt, bird

droppings, tree sap, and other debris. To clean them, take them down and bring them outside. Lay them flat on an old blanket or fabric dropcloth so that they won't bulge or be scratched during cleaning. Scrub them with a brush and some all-purpose cleaner solution. Rinse with a hose. Rap them with your hand to shake the loose water off when you're through, and dry them in the sun.

474 Plexiglas

Before you try to clean Plexiglas, be sure to rinse it well with water. Plexiglas attracts dust, and you can be sure there will be some on the surface—rinse it away before it has a chance to be caught underneath your cleaning cloth, where it will cause scratches.

475 Short cut

If you're busy and must skip something, forget about cleaning the windows. Glass is a nondepreciable material. It doesn't become damaged or worn from dirt, no matter how dirty it gets. Carpet is a different story. When carpet stays dirty, it literally wears out.

476 A clean deal

Venetian blinds, because they have so many horizontal surfaces, are like the top of the fridge when it comes to collecting grease, dust, and insect residue. They can be dusted and vacuumed in place, but for real deep cleaning they have to be taken down. Put them in the closed position and lay them on an old blanket or tarp that has been put down on a slanted or inclined surface such as a driveway. Scrub the blinds with a soft brush and ammonia solution; then turn them over and do the other side. Rinse them with the hose, and then shake them to reduce water spots. This method sure beats doing them in a tub or in place!

477 All that's not fit to blot

Contrary to popular opinion, drying windows with newspaper will leave an ink residue that can dull the shine of the glass and even transfer to drapes. Squeegee your windows, and you won't have to dry them with anything!

478 Try a squeegee

How are the windows on commercial buildings kept so sparkling clean? With a squeegee—a few quick strokes and you're finished. You can get a professional quality squeegee in a variety of useful sizes and instructions on its use at a janitorial supply store. You will probably find that squeegees are quicker, cheaper, and kind of fun.

479 Hold the soap, please!

The number one, most frequent mistake people make when cleaning windows is using too much cleaner or too heavy a concentration of cleaner in the washing water, which results in streaks. Window-squeegeeing solution needs some cleaner to make it slippery, but just a little—just enough to break the surface tension of the glass. Dishwashing detergent works great for this, but a couple of drops in a bucket is enough. Attack any stuck-on matter with a separate bowl or bucket of more concentrated cleaner.

480 Window wand

How do pros loosen and remove all that dirt and grit from windows before squeegeeing? Not with an old T-shirt or wadded up newspaper but with a real or synthetic lambswool washing wand that fits on the end of an extension handle. You can get one at a janitorial supply store. It'll clean even the tallest windows with ease.

481 Extension handle

Second-story windows can be done easily with a squeegee on an extension handle, and your feet will never leave the ground. With an extension handle (aluminum is good), no ladder is needed, and there's no safety risk. A four-foot handle that extends to eight feet is the best all-around size for the average home.

482 Professional recipe

The window-cleaning solution most of us pros use when squeegeeing glass is simply a few drops of

Dawn or other dishwashing detergent in a bucket of water. That's right, only a few drops! Try it if you don't believe me.

483 How to squeegee

Always wipe your squeegee blade between strokes with a damp cloth, not a dry one. The damp cloth will remove excess water, yet leave the blade lubricated so that it won't twitch and jig when it hits a dry place on the glass.

484 Nicked squeegee blade

If the rubber blade on your squeegee gets nicked, you can turn it around and use the other side. When the whole blade gets blunt and rounded, it's time to replace it. Don't put it off. A nicked blade will leave streaks, adding unecessary minutes to your cleaning time.

485 Sun streaks

Never wash windows in direct sunlight if you can possibly avoid it. The sun dries the solution too fast and leaves ugly streaks on the glass that will have to be cleaned off. If you have to wash windows in bright sunlight, be extra sure not to put too much cleaner in the water and squeegee *fast*!

486 Gunky spray

Creamy glass cleaners often contain wax that builds up on windows and actually make them dirtier over a period of time. Glass cleaned with sticky products like these will streak and get dirty more quickly because it attracts dust and dirt. For quick, small jobs (when you don't want to drag out your squeegee and bucket), use a spray bottle with an alcohol-based, evaporating window cleaner such as Windex; then polish with a cleaning cloth.

487 Water mark

To remove water spots left when drips dry, use your bare hand or finger and nothing else. By the time you've done a few windows, the cleaning solution will have cleaned the skin oil off your hands, and there's no better tool for removing marks and drips from the glass.

488 Bug collection?

For those window tracks that become a sticky insect burial site, I loosen the bug collection with an old toothbrush and then vacuum with a special crevice attachment. If the track is wet and mucky from the moisture of condensation, or if debris is dried on and hard, I spray on some all-purpose cleaning solution and let it sit for five minutes. Then I wrap the blade of a screwdriver with a small piece of terry cloth and run the blade down the track. Most of the muck sticks to the terry cloth. Repeat with clean cloth if necessary.

489 Jalousies

To clean jalousies or slatted windows, a six-inch tweezers-like squeegee has been invented that works a little better than the spray bottle and rag routine. You just wipe dish detergent solution on the slats and then squeegee it off one slat at a time and wipe with a dry cloth.

490 Hard water buildup

Hard water deposits on windows are simply a buildup of minerals (usually lime or calcium) from the water. The longer it's on a window, the tougher it is to get off. We pros use a phosphoric acid cleaner like Showers 'N Stuff to remove it. You can get professional-strength phosphoric acid from a janitorial supply store. Wipe it on, wait for it to dissolve the scale, and then rinse it off.

491 Gummed glass

Labels, stickers, and their sticky residue that stays behind on glass can be taken off with either a razor blade scraper, or a heavy duty solvent like De-Solv-it, which melts and dissolves the heavy duty, really sticky stuff. Always wet the window first if you intend to use a scraper and work carefully to avoid scratches.

492 Scraping

Scraping something off a window? A plain old razor blade in a hand holder is still the best method I've found. But always wet the glass first so that it'll be less likely to scratch. Always scrape with a "push" stroke, lifting the blade from the glass before bringing it back. Pulling a blade backward on the glass can trap sand or dirt under the blade and actually etch the glass.

493 Squeegee or spray bottle?

For small decorative panes on doors or windows, use a spray bottle of fast-evaporating window cleaner and a soft cloth. For anything over two feet square, use a squeegee—it's faster and does a better job.

WOOD FLOORS

494 Wood opinion

People disagree about the best way to care for wood floors. I make sure they have a good varnish or polyurethane finish on them; then I wax, buff, and clean them just like any other hard-surface.

495 The test

To tell if your wood floor needs cleaning or finish, wet the end of your finger and touch a section of the area to be cleaned. If the spot darkens immediately, the finish has worn off. If the hue of the wood stays about the same, your problem is dirt and wax buildup...clean it!

496 Wet mopping wood

It may not show much, but wood floors get dirty and tacky and need to be cleaned. When they do get dirty, damp mop with all-purpose cleaner solution. Water doesn't hurt a varnished or polyurethaned wood floor if you get the water on and off fast and don't let it form a pool or sit there.

497 Those crevices!

Older wood floors may have almost invisible cracks in the finish, especially between the boards. These will collect dirt and eventually allow moisture to seep in to warp the floor. You'll want to be sure that a floor like this receives a fresh coat of varnish or polyurethane periodically.

498 Vacuum wood?

When you have to use a lot of solution to scrub badly soiled wood floors, use a wet/dry vacuum right behind the floor scrubber (hand or machine). It gets the moisture up quicker and better than a mop or even a floor squeegee.

499 Knot smart!

Vacuum wood floors carefully. The floor brush on a canister is okay, but any upright or canister power wand with a brush roll can toss a pebble or piece of gravel into the surface and chip it, and a vacuum beater bar can dent a wood floor. A treated dust mop is the best tool for sweeping wood floors.

500 Wood wisdom

Don't sand ugly wood floors. Sanding leaves floor boards a little thinner. Most of the ugliness can be attributed to old, darkened finish. A paint and varnish stripper will remove it. After you've applied the stripper and given it a chance to work, squeegee off the gunk; then level the floor, using a sanding screen on a buffer. When it's dry, apply one coat of sealer and two coats of polyurethane or varnish.

INDEX

159

160